my ART book

DK PUBLISHING

Contents

LONDON, NEW YORK,
MELBOURNE, MUNICH, and DELHI

Senior designer Sonia Moore
Senior editor Deborah Lock
Additional design by Rosie Levine, Laura Roberts-Jensen, Lauren Rosier, Hedi Hunter, Gemma Fletcher, Poppy Joslin
Additional editing by Lorrie Mack
Photographer Will Heap
Art consultant Ian Chilvers
US editor Margaret Parrish

Category publisher Mary Ling
Picture researcher Jo Walton
Production editor Andy Hilliard
Production controller Claire Pearson
Jacket designer Martin Wilson
Jacket editor Matilda Gollon

First published in the United States in 2011
by DK Publishing
375 Hudson Street, New York, New York 10014

11 12 13 14 15 10 9 8 7 6 5 4 3 2 1
179460—02/2011

A catalog record for this book
is available from the Library of Congress.
ISBN 978-0-7566-7582-0

Color reproduction by MDP, UK
Printed and bound by Toppan, China

Discover more at
www.dk.com

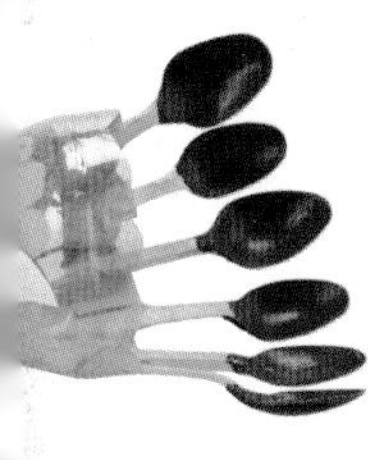

Let's get creative!

Scale

In order to show how large or small a piece of art is we have compared it to this hand or boy.

The hand is 5 in (12 cm) high.

The boy is 43 in (110 cm) tall.

My art studio

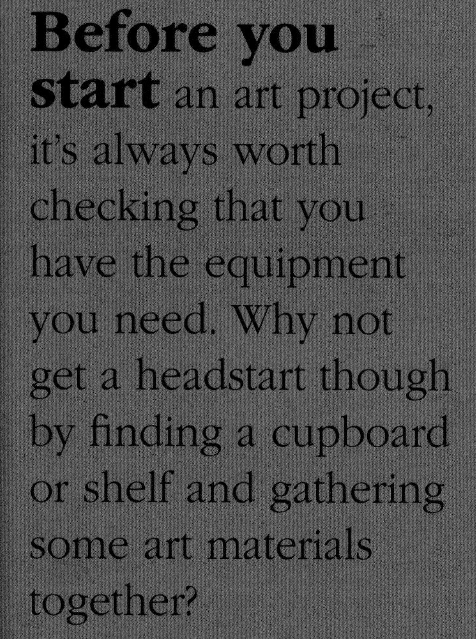

Before you start an art project, it's always worth checking that you have the equipment you need. Why not get a headstart though by finding a cupboard or shelf and gathering some art materials together?

Watercolor paints

Poster paints

Tubes of acrylic paint

Craft glue

You'll need different-sized brushes to paint with, and pencils are handy for sketching your pictures first.

Paint-brushes

Pencils and crayons

Pens

Recycle

Keep a supply of interestingly shaped recycled bottles, boxes, and odds and ends from your home, as well as natural objects you've collected on a walk or from a beach.

Materials

Collect construction paper and cardboard in different shades and textures. The projects in this book also use plain cardboard, transparencies, leather, and tracing paper.

Animal magic

ONE SEPTEMBER AFTERNOON in 1940, four boys (and a dog named Robot) were exploring caves in southwest France. Suddenly, they found wonderful pictures on the walls. These paintings—of animals, people, and mysterious symbols—had been hidden for thousands and thousands of years.

Cave paintings,
17,000 BCE,
found in Lascaux, France

Early record

On this wall of the cave, the paintings show horselike creatures (not exactly like modern horses) and cattle.

Many more horselike animals, stags, and cattle appear on other walls of the cave, plus cats and birds, a bear, and a rhinoceros. But there are no caribou—this is odd, because scientists believe that the people who made these paintings ate more caribou meat than any other kind.

The paintings are this big!

Black bulls

Some of the most famous Lascaux images are bulls that seem to be running very fast—and they look just like modern bison in North America and Europe. Most of the bull paintings are in one place, which is called the "Hall of Bulls."

The paintings are this big!

Hunting for answers

We think all the cave images are about hunting—they may record past hunts, or they may be part of a ritual to improve future hunts. Or maybe they're just decoration—we just don't know.

Colors from nature

These artists drew with burned wood or bone (charcoal), ash, ground-up minerals (such as ocher clay), or color from plants, probably mixed with water. Experts think the "paint" was applied with moss or fur pads, or directly onto the wall, using solid lumps of pigment (color) as if they were crayons.

Ash

Charcoal

Make *a cave painting*

Collect these things together before you begin.

Creating colors

My art project

1 Crush the berries. Using a stick, mix with a little water to make a smooth red paste.

2 Mix the dark soil with a spoonful of lard. Add more soil to make the "paint" darker and less greasy or more lard if the paint is too dry.

3 Using the roof tile as a slab, crush the chalk with a stone, grinding it to a powder. Mix this powder with water to make a white paste.

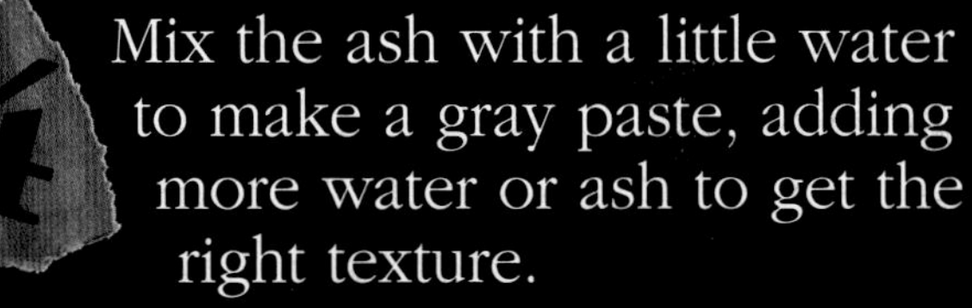

4 Mix the ash with a little water to make a gray paste, adding more water or ash to get the right texture.

Caveman painting

5 With charcoal or a burned stick, draw the bison's body on your floor tile. Use simple lines and straight-sided shapes.

6 Draw a triangle with stick horns for the head, and add a stick man in front of the animal, running away.

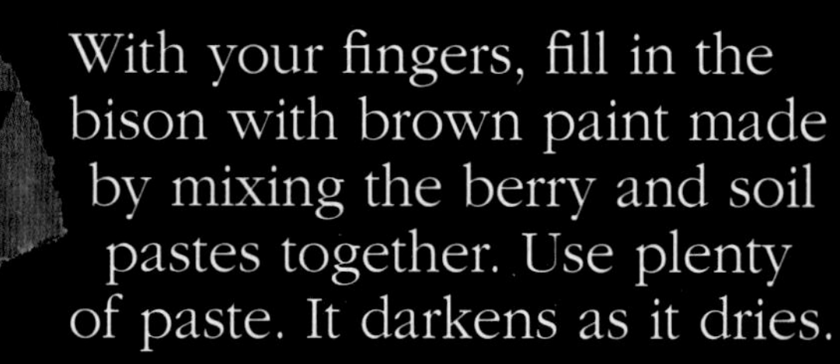

7 With your fingers, fill in the bison with brown paint made by mixing the berry and soil pastes together. Use plenty of paste. It darkens as it dries.

8 Mix the chalk and ash pastes. Smudge this onto parts of the face and the back to highlight these areas, so that the bison stands out.

Use a charcoal stick to darken the hooves and the end of the tail.

My art project

Try drawing onto a piece of leather, using ash, chalk, and charcoal.

Mount your picture by stapling the leather onto a piece of cardboard. Cut straight edges, or rip them to give a rough, natural look.

Display your work on a shelf.

Dreaming dots

Wirrimanu
by a community of Balgo woman, **1999,** made with acrylic paint on canvas

The **AUSTRALIAN ABORIGINAL PEOPLE** have been creating art for many thousands of years. Today, artists continue to tell stories about their culture and land through their work.

Can you find these symbols?

Many of the symbols in "Dreaming" paintings have hidden meanings or religious importance.

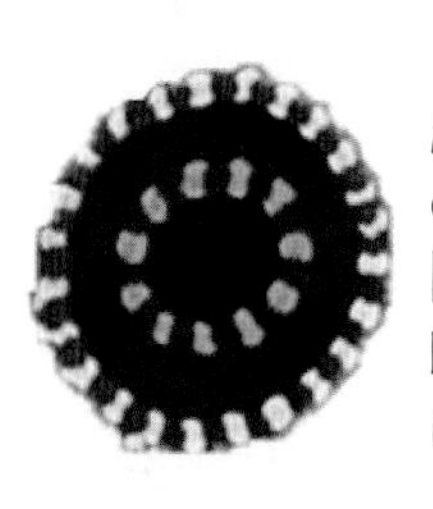

A waterhole created by the Kingfisher when he put his beak into the ground.

A bush potato that the people gathered to eat.

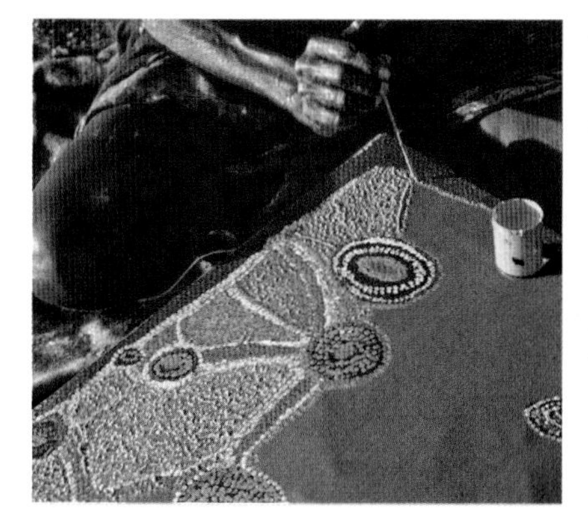

The artists of the Balgo community use the technique of dot painting.

The Balgo community

The Balgo community is found in the Western Desert of Western Australia. Wirrimanu is the native name for the Balgo Hills area.

Balgo Hills

Artist

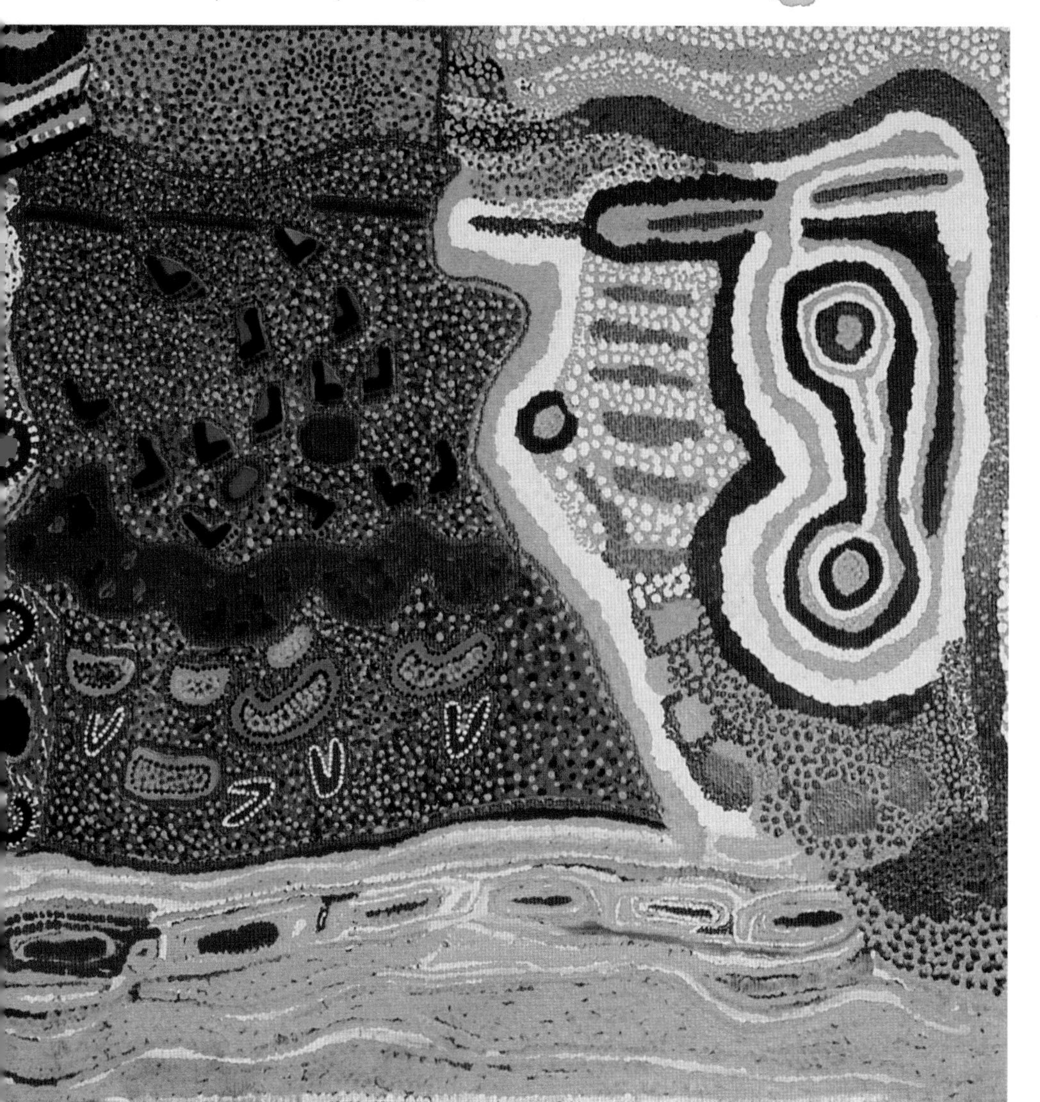

A story in pictures

This painting is a "Dreaming" story about the Luurnpa, or Kingfisher, who formed the creeks of Wirrimanu and provided the people with water and food. The lines and dots are used as symbols to tell the story.

The painting is this big!

The creeks that flow across the land, created by the Kingfisher.

The people gathered together by the Kingfisher around the waterholes.

A wooden bowl filled with food by the people.

Decorate a rock

Gather this equipment together before you begin.

1 Using a pencil, sketch the outline of a lizard or another Australian animal onto the rock.

2 Use orange paint for the background around the shape. Allow this to dry, then fill in the animal with a suitable color—green for a lizard.

3 Once this is dry, make a line of white dots all around the shape you've made. Now fill in the background with lots of bright, multicolored dots, continuing to go around the shape of the animal.

Paint on eyes.

Add varnish for a shiny finish.

Next, make lines of yellow dots inside the animal shape, and along its legs (if it has legs). Add a red dot inside each yellow dot to finish the pattern.

Artist

African masks

Some **AFRICAN** tribes use **MASKS** to link the real world with the world of spirits and the dead. Masks are often worn for ceremonial dances.

Bwoom

The Kuba tribe uses three main masks in its religious ceremonies—this one shows a figure named Bwoom, who usually represents the ordinary man.

Simple patterns like this are common in Kuba art.

The mask is this big!

African mask
Kuba tribe, **1800s,**
made with painted wood and straw

Other African masks...

Masks are meant to show character, rather than real faces. To make a mask, the sculptor cuts off a chunk of wood and leaves it to dry in the Sun. When it's ready, he carves the features.

Mbuya masks, made by the Pende people of the Democratic Republic of the Congo, were worn for harvest and hunting ceremonies, and other festivities. The long beard suggests power and wisdom.

The Dan people on the Ivory Coast carve masks that have a high forehead and a line that divides the nose and forehead in two.

This line symbolizes the two parts of the world—human and spiritual.

Feathers make a bushy beard.

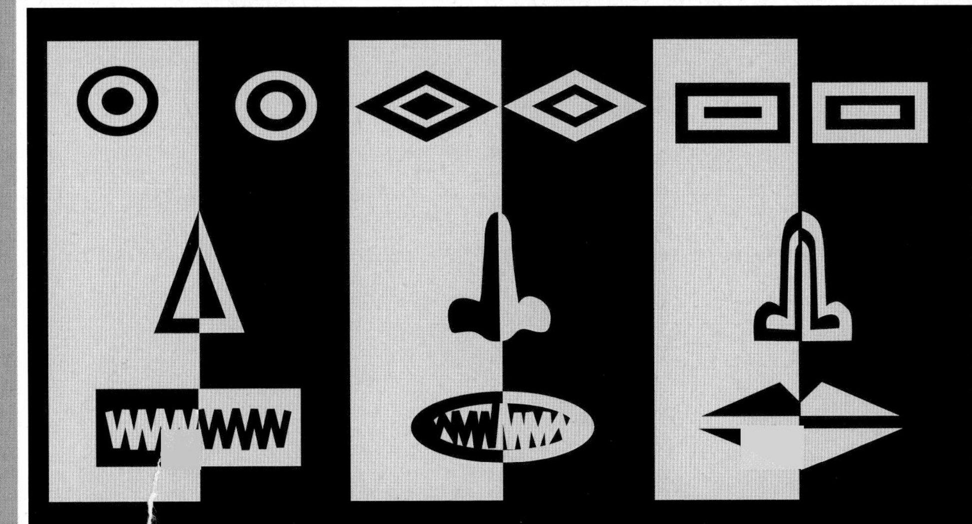

Fine features

The sculptor chooses the shape of the mask's eyes, nose, and mouth. He picks them out in black charcoal, or colored powder made from plants or minerals. Which one will you choose for the project on page 19?

Make *a mask*

Gather this equipment together before you begin.

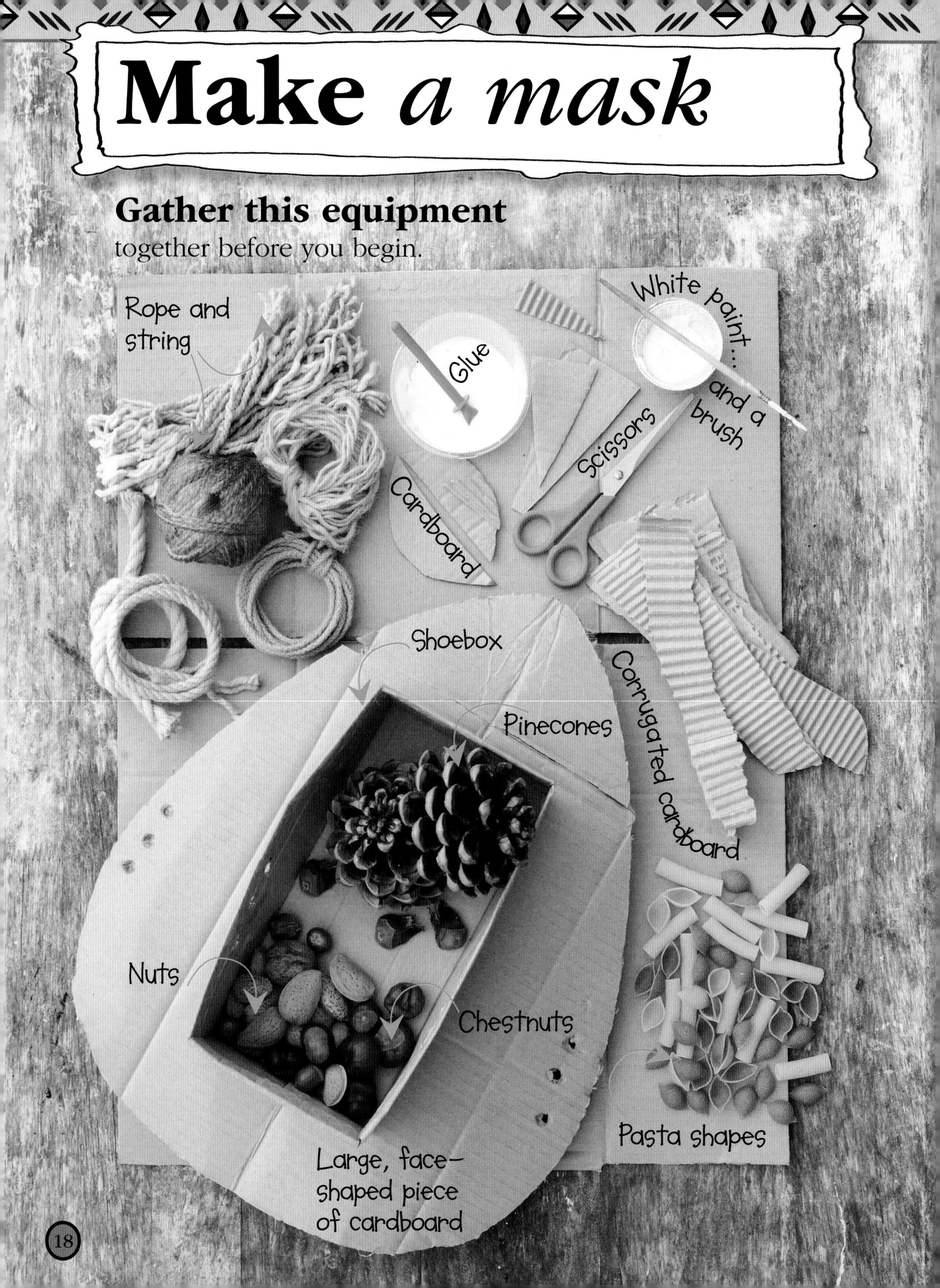

Tip: Cut long pieces of string; use them to tie the mask onto your head.

1 Ask an adult to make three holes on each side of the shoebox and the face-shaped cardboard. Thread string through to attach them together.

2 For the mouth and nose, cut out and glue down pieces of cardboard in different sizes—the smallest on top. The layers make the nose stick out.

3 Do the same thing for the eyes, gluing down two or three layers of cardboard. Try making eyebrows out of big seeds or nuts.

4 For the hair, make holes at the top of the face, and thread long pieces of string or rope through each one. Tie a knot to secure the "hair."

Glue nuts onto the corrugated cardboard.

Corrugated cardboard looks like combed hair.

Make a headband with pasta shapes.

Add warrior markings* with white paint.

Glue on ears made from cardboard.

Make earrings from string and a chestnut.

Use corrugated cardboard around the edge of the face.

My art project
Mask gallery
Make a cardboard-box monster mask with a paper-towel tube neck bolt.
Create a pussycat mask with a brown bag and paper whiskers.
Use chestnuts for bulging eyes, and tie on string hair.
Go for glamour with feathers and painted red lips.
Cut up an old string mop to make floppy bangs.
Dangle paper "corks" from a folded hat to make an Australian mask.
For a beard, cut paper in strips and curl them with a scissor blade.
Use pieces of curled paper to create whiskers and eyelashes.

Fantastic faces

Vertumnus (Portrait of Rudolf II) by Giuseppe Arcimboldo, **1590,** made with oil paint on a wood panel

Born in Italy, **GIUSEPPE ARCIMBOLDO** (*c.* 1527–93) could paint ordinary pictures, but he's best known for his weird faces made up of plants and animals.

Main meaning

Arcimboldo linked his materials to his subject. This portrait (right) shows the emperor Rudolf II as *Vertumnus,* Roman god of orchards. In it, crops and flowers suggests the health and plenty of his reign.

Rudolf II (1552–1612), Holy Roman Emperor, painted by Hans von Aachen

Let's zoom in closer...

There are lots of different fruits, vegetables, and flowers in this amazing portrait, and they represent all four seasons. When you look very carefully, can you find...

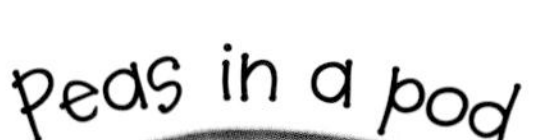

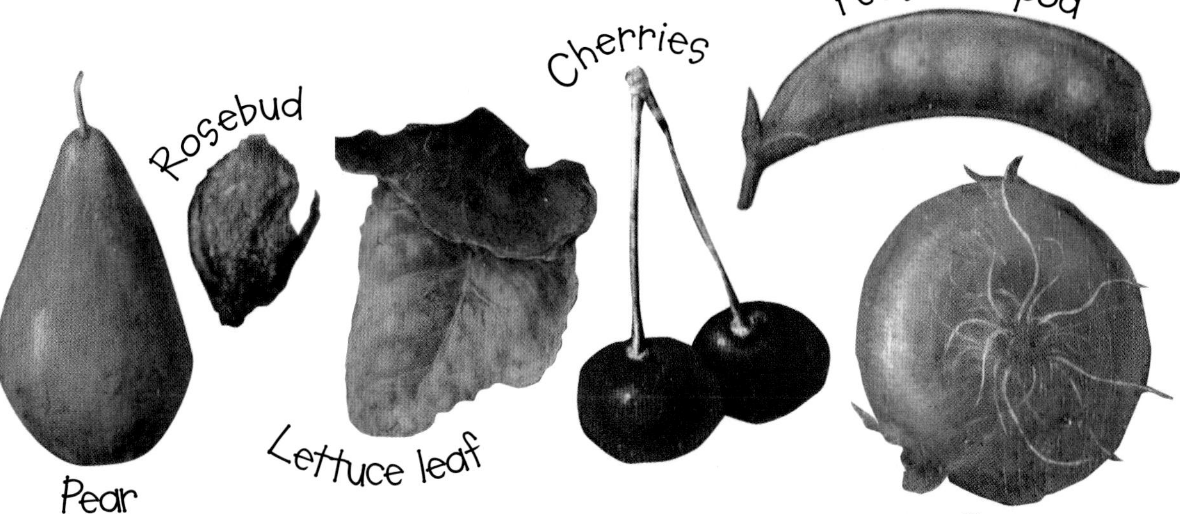

Arcimboldo also painted...

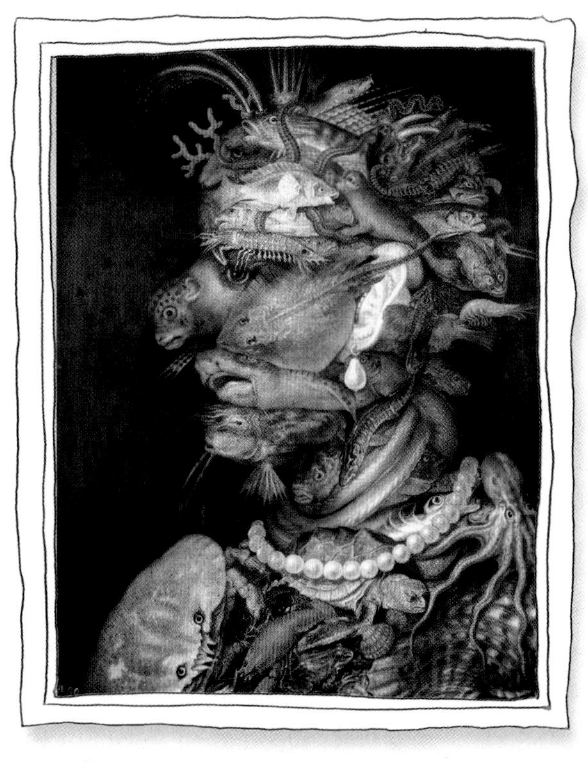

***Water*, 1566**
Arcimboldo made pictures of the four elements—earth, air, fire, and water. This one is full of sea creatures—how many can you see?

***The Vegetable Gardener*, 1580**
When you turn this portrait of a farmer upside down, it becomes a bowlful of ripe vegetables.

Make *a face*

Gather these things before you begin.

Look at the different shapes and textures.

1 On a large piece of dark cardboard (or a trash bag), create a head shape, using a layer of large green leaves for the face and curly ones for the hair.

2 Place large pieces of fruit and vegetable around the cheeks, in the hair, and around the neck.

3 Add handfuls of smaller fruits and vegetables to build up the face. Use darker pieces, such as blueberries, for the parts of the face in shade.

Scallions make a bushy moustache.

For each eye, cut an avocado in half, and put snow peas around the pit.

Remember to take a photograph of your fantastic face before you take it apart. Frame it!

... making more fun faces? Look around your home and find other things you could use, such as shiny pieces of metal or plastic toys.

My art project

Edible profile

Mr. Metal Head

Frame the photographs of your faces, or print them and use to make greeting cards.

Fabulous fall

Plastic fantastic

Dragons and *heroes*

The Great Wave of Kanagawa
by Katsushika Hokusai,
1829–1833,
woodblock print

KATSUSHIKA HOKUSAI (1760–1849) is the most famous of all Japanese artists. Like most of them, he showed history and legends, but he put ordinary people and scenes in his pictures, too.

In this box, Hokusai has signed his name. He used more than 20 different names throughout his career, and produced more than 30,000 works in all.

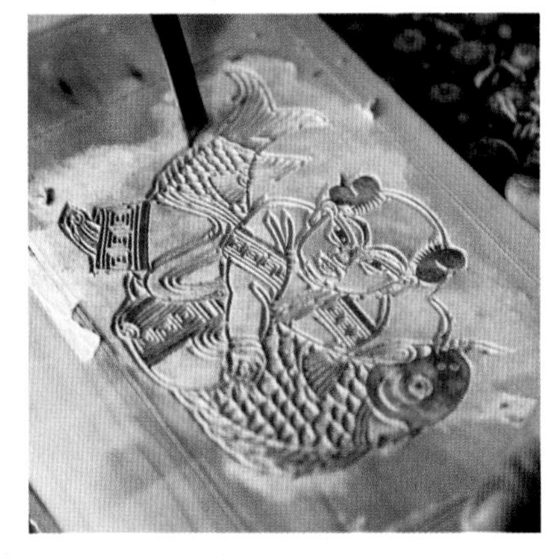
A chisel carves shapes into the wooden printing blocks.

Block printing

This technique has been used in Japan for centuries. The artist cuts a design into a smooth block of wood and prints it onto paper. A different block is used for each color, and lots of copies can be made from the same blocks.

Mount Fuji

In the background, framed by the biggest wave, is Mount Fuji, the highest peak in Japan. In legend, this mountain is the home of the gods.

The waves have curly spikes at the end that look like sharp claws.

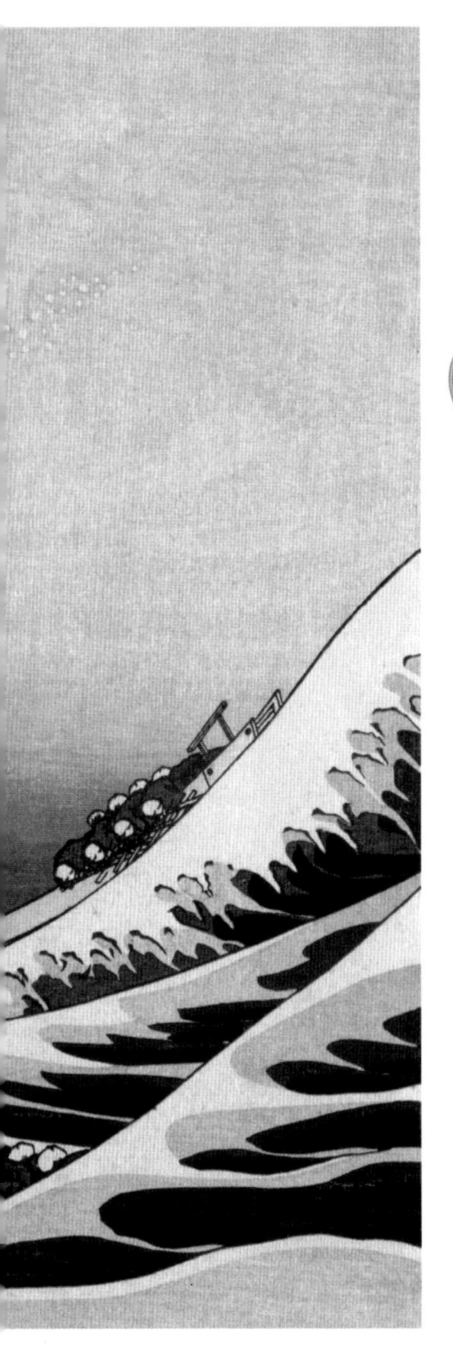

Zoom in...

These fishermen are taking their catch home in small boats, when they are caught in the huge waves. Do they look scared or excited?

The print is this big!

Hokusai also printed...

Hokusai has used the same spiked wave pattern as a sort of round, painted frame on this dragon canopy for a festival float. There are lots of dragons in Japanese art and culture, and most are like this—big snakelike creatures with no wings and huge claws.

Dragon canopy, 1830

Print a picture

Gather this equipment

together before you begin.

Polystyrene pizza base

Acrylic paints

Masking tape

You will cut up offcuts from the pizza base for the "L" markers.

Roller

Teaspoon

Pencil

Soft foam sponge

Tracing paper

Red paper

Tip: Trace the dragon template at the end of the book, or design one of your own.

1 Draw a dragon onto tracing paper. To transfer your shape onto the pizza base, punch holes through the tracing paper and join them together.

2 Using the end of a teaspoon, press down firmly around the outline of the dragon. Cut the pizza base into a square shape, saving the offcuts.

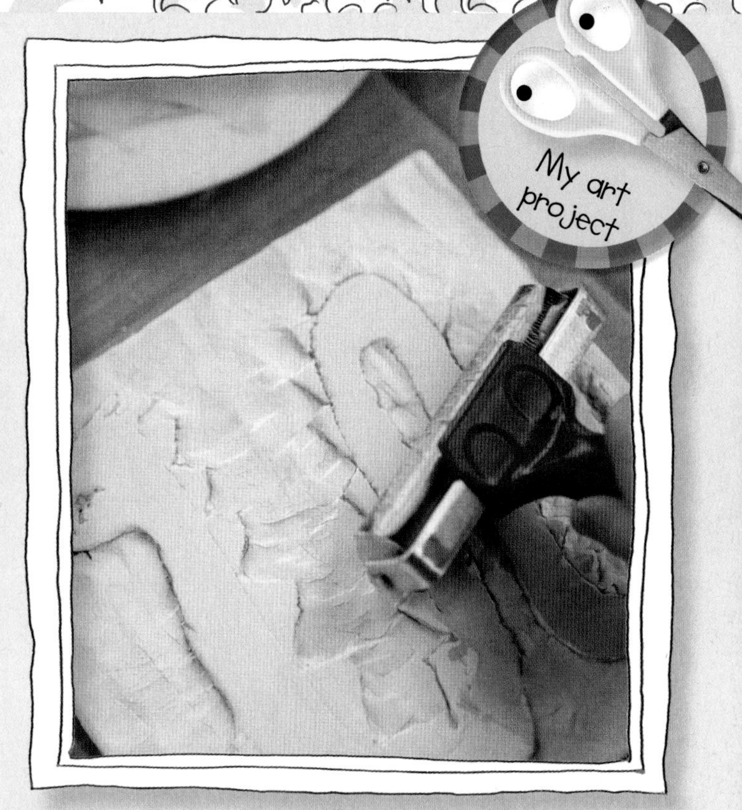

3 Place the base onto the red paper and mark the corners with small L-shaped brackets cut from the waste. Stick them down with masking tape.

4 Ink up the dragon shape on the pizza base using yellow paint on a roller. Acrylic paint dries fast, so try to work quickly.

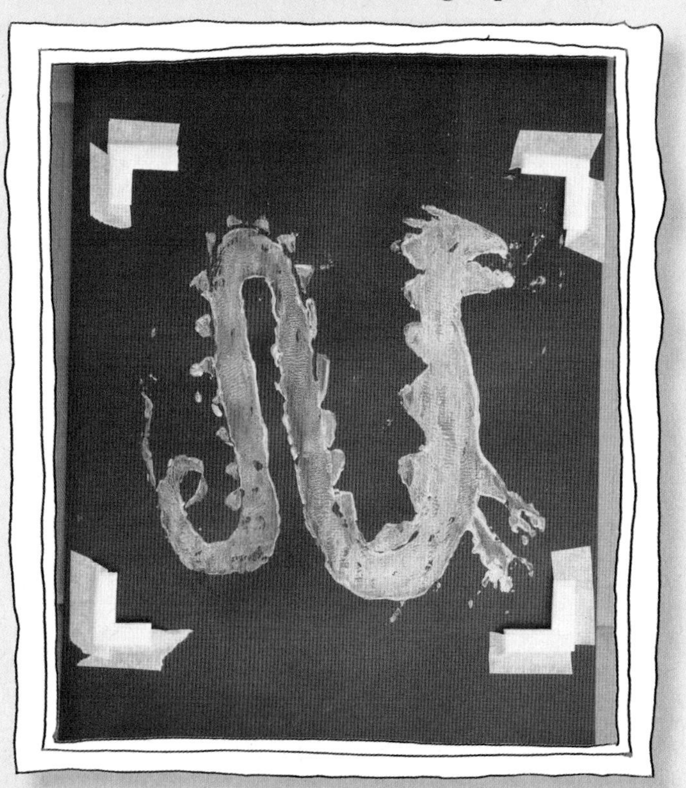

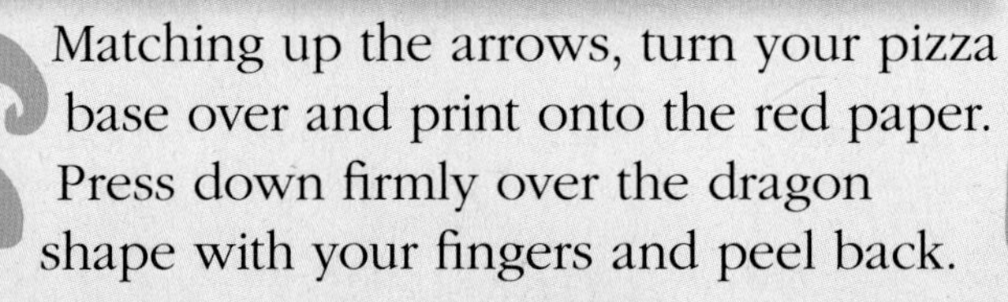

5 Matching up the arrows, turn your pizza base over and print onto the red paper. Press down firmly over the dragon shape with your fingers and peel back.

6 Wipe the paint off the dragon, then draw the U-shaped scales along its body. To make these lines, press down hard with a pencil.

7 Ink up the dragon again, this time using green paint on the roller. If you get paint on the areas that aren't raised, wipe it off with a wet cloth.

8 Turn the pizza base over. Using the corner markers and arrows as a guide, place it onto the dragon shape on the red paper. Press firmly.

... pressing down just the outline of your dragon instead of all the background?

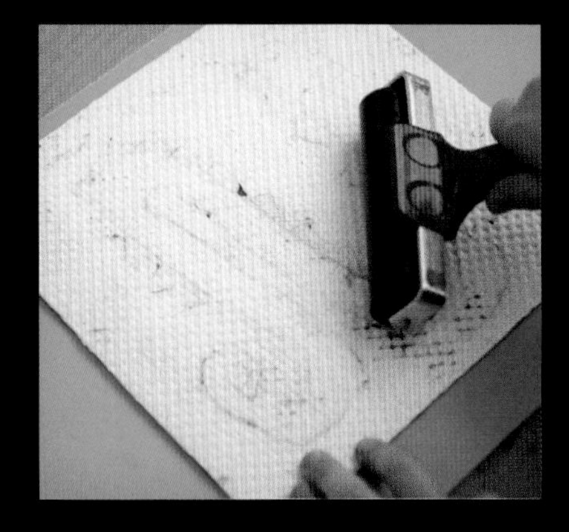

Draw the outline of your dragon shape, pressing down in the lines.

Ink up using a roller, then cover the whole picture.

Turn it over onto a piece of paper and press it down using a roller.

Use gold candy wrappers for the dragon's fiery breath.

To finish, cut the red paper into a square shape and mount your picture onto black cardboard.

Frame it!

Wipe the pizza base clean. Draw on the dragon's scales and press down in these lines with the pencil.

Peel the picture away carefully to see the printed background.

Ink up in another color and print on top of your picture again.

Freeze *frame*

Star Dancer
by Edgar Degas, **1876,**
made with pastel on paper

Edgar Degas (1834–1917) is famous for his paintings of ballet dancers. He also produced wonderful pictures of horse racing, circuses, and ladies bathing and getting dressed.

Let's zoom in closer...

As Degas got older, his sight failed, and he began using pastels. He liked their smudgy effect (it looked like what he could see), and they were easy to blend. He could afford to experiment—he was rich, so it didn't matter if he sold his work or not.

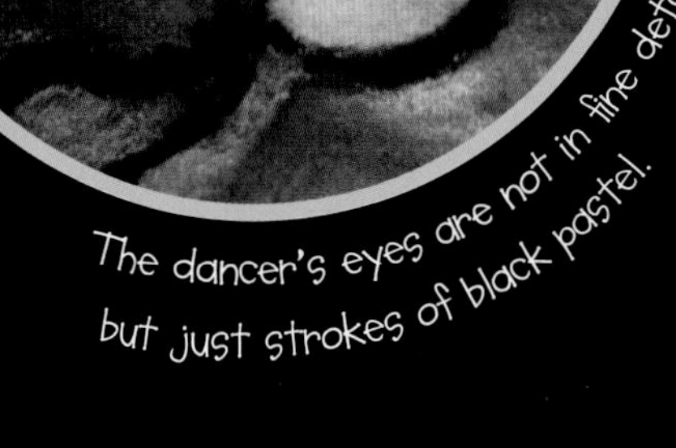

The dancer's eyes are not in fine detail but just strokes of black pastel.

Trick of the light

Degas shows this ballerina at the moment she takes her bow. From his position high above her (maybe in an expensive theater box), the net of her tutu seems to dissolve in the strong stage lights.

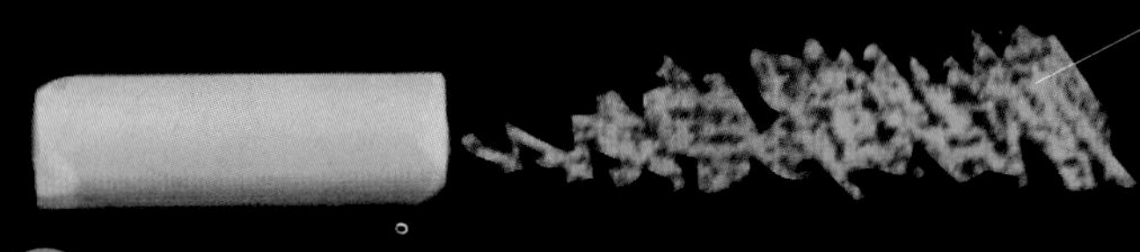

Pastels are made from powder pigment (color) mixed with sticky gum to form crayonlike sticks.

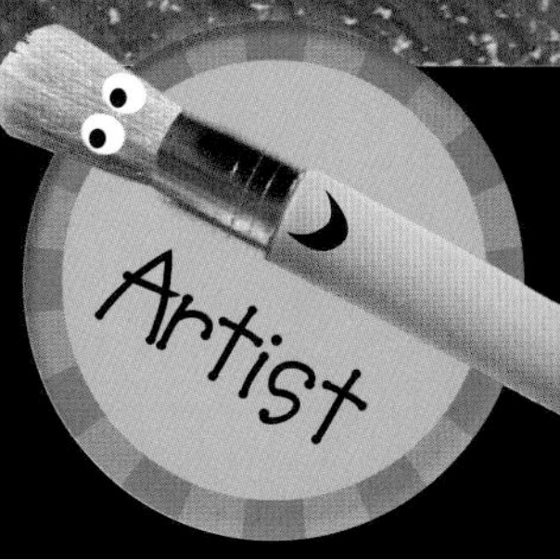

Degas' images appear to capture a fleeting moment—as if he dashed off sketches on the spot. In fact, he composed all his pictures very carefully.

Degas also painted...

Jockeys in the Rain, 1886
Whether he was painting dancers or horses, Degas was an expert at expressing movement.

Miss La La at the Cirque Fernando, 1879
Degas was fascinated by photography. He often captured his subjects from unexpected angles, like a camera might.

Paint *with pastels*

Gather these things together before you begin.

1 Sketch out your dancer using a pastel color that is slightly darker than the paper. Start at the highest point and work down the body.

2 Use dark green, blue, and brown pastels to fill the background. Use short, quick marks all made in the same direction, away from the dancer.

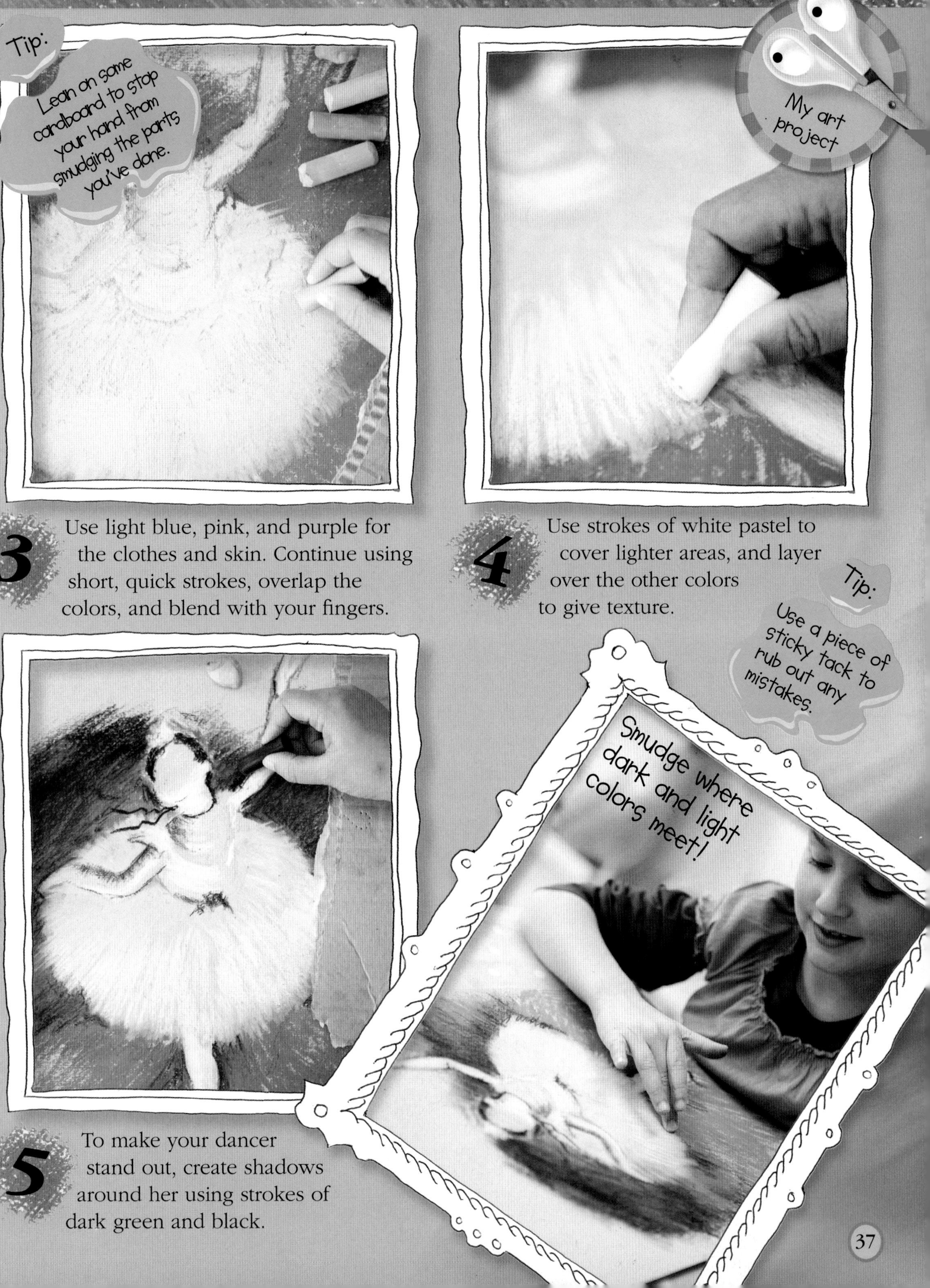

3 Use light blue, pink, and purple for the clothes and skin. Continue using short, quick strokes, overlap the colors, and blend with your fingers.

4 Use strokes of white pastel to cover lighter areas, and layer over the other colors to give texture.

5 To make your dancer stand out, create shadows around her using strokes of dark green and black.

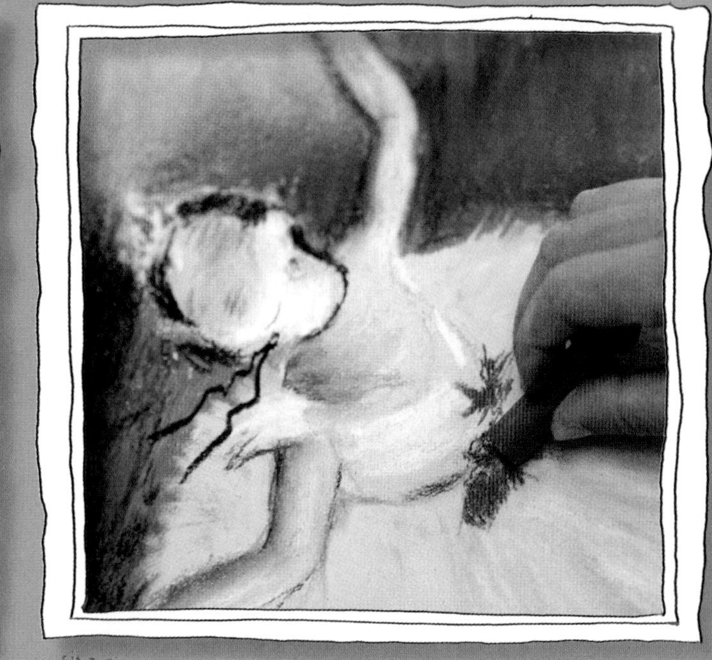

5 Around the legs and arms, blend the dark edges with a rolled-up piece of paper. This is more accurate than smudging with your finger.

6 To finish, add short red strokes for flowers on the dancer's dress and hairpiece. Spray a fixative over the painting to prevent further smudging.

Sidewalk painting

My art project

YOU WILL NEED

Cornstarch
Food coloring
Cold water
Paintbrushes
Small pots
Spoon

HOW TO MAKE THE PAINT

1

Put a tablespoon of cornstarch and a cup of cold water into a small pot. Mix until the cornstarch dissolves. Prepare the mixture in other small pots in the same way.

2

For each color, add a few drops of the chosen food coloring to one of the pots. Follow the steps for the smaller picture, but enlarge to a bigger scale. Use separate paintbrushes for each color.

Homemade chalk paint

Chalk pastels

Remember to take a photograph before cleaning your picture off the sidewalk with a hose.

SwiSheS and SwirlS

Starry Night
by Vincent van Gogh, **1889,**
was made with oil paint on canvas. He was in a mental hospital in France at the time.

VINCENT VAN GOGH (1853–1890), born in the Netherlands, sold few paintings while he was alive. After his death, he became one of the most famous and admired artists who ever lived.

Troubled mind

Van Gogh taught himself to draw and paint. He worked incredibly hard and produced hundreds of pictures, but he was very unhappy, and sometimes felt as if he were losing his mind.

Let's zoom in closer...

The paint in this picture is put on the canvas in thick, bright swirls. Do you think the artist felt calm and happy when he was painting it? Or was he upset and worried?

When you look at the night sky, you don't see white and bright colors. But van Gogh used them in his picture to show how the sky made him feel.

Van Gogh liked to use a fat brush loaded with paint. He made thick brushstrokes, and sometimes even squeezed paint straight out of the tube.

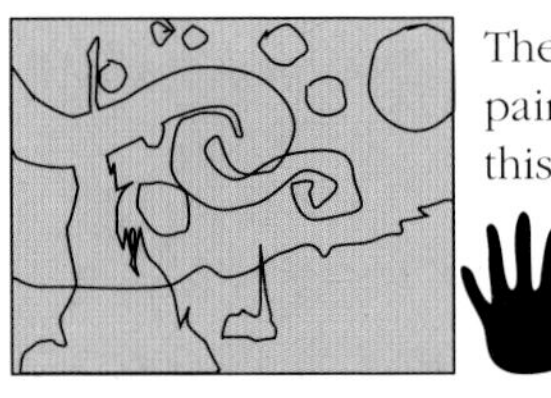

The painting is this big!

Artist

Van Gogh also painted...

Sunflowers, 1888
One of the most famous paintings in the world, ***Sunflowers*** shows some flowers in full bloom and others wilted and dying.

Sunflowers by Oscar, age 10
Since van Gogh, many other artists have been inspired to do their own version of the ***Sunflowers***. Why not try it, too?

Paint *a night sky*

Gather this equipment

together before you begin.

1 Plan your picture by making a light pencil sketch on your cardboard. Load a brush with lots of dark-blue paint and swirl around for the sky.

2 For the stars, choose a lighter shade of blue paint. Load it thickly on the brush and swirl it around in circles.

3 For the hills and town, use dark green and blue paint. Short strokes of light blue will suggest buildings.

4 Use light and dark shades of green for the big tree. Continue to paint with short, swirly strokes.

Swirl yellow and white paint on the stars and Moon to make them bright and sparkly.

Use blobs of yellow paint for the lighted windows in your houses.

Jungle fantasy

Tiger in a Tropical Storm
by Henri Rousseau, **1891,**
made with oil paint on canvas

HENRI ROUSSEAU (1844–1910) painted wild animals in the jungle. But he never saw a jungle—he just used familiar plants and made them bigger!

Out and about

Rousseau taught himself to paint. He lived in the city of Paris, France, and often visited the zoo and nearby botanical gardens. He sketched the animals and tropical plants there, then used these sketches to create his paintings—they're not real jungle scenes.

Look closer

Look at the tiger's face with its large frightened eyes and open mouth. What's scared him? Is it the thunder and lightning? Is he leaping away to find somewhere to shelter from the heavy rain of the tropical storm?

The painting is this big!

Simple shapes

Rousseau noticed that many leaves are *symmetrical*—when they're split in half, the two sides are the same. He made his paintings interesting by using different colors for the leaves.

Rousseau also painted...

Compare this picture with a photograph of a tropical jungle. Which plants shouldn't really be here?

Exotic Landscape, 1910

Create *a collage jungle*

1 Begin with the background. Tear a strip of blue for the sky and one of brown for the soil, and glue these onto your white background paper.

2 From brown paper, cut out a tree with a bent trunk and branches. Glue it down. For shading, add a line of yellow pastel along the tops of the branches.

3 Accordion-fold some green paper and cut out a few symmetrical leaf shapes for your tree. Now shade each one by edging it with yellow pastel and smudging it with your finger.

4 Glue the leaves onto the tree. Draw, then cut out, an animal. Add details to its face and body using pastel pencils. Glue it on.

5 For the foreground, cut out and shade long blades of grass and plants with big leaves. Glue these down, placing them over the animal.

To make your shapes stand out, draw around them with black pencil.

Cut out simple flowers.

Musical painting

Composition 7
by Wassily Kandinsky, **1913,**
made with oil paint on canvas

Russian painter **WASSILY KANDINSKY** (1866-1944) was one of the first people to paint pictures that are known as "abstract" art. He was a musician as well as an artist.

But what is abstract art?

At one time, art always showed realistic people or things. But Kandinsky and other abstract artists thought that pure painting was only about colors and shapes. He also believed that abstract art could express just as much feeling as music.

Artist

"Compositions" is a term that refers to pieces of music as well as paintings. Kandinsky created 10 pictures in his series called "*Compositions*."

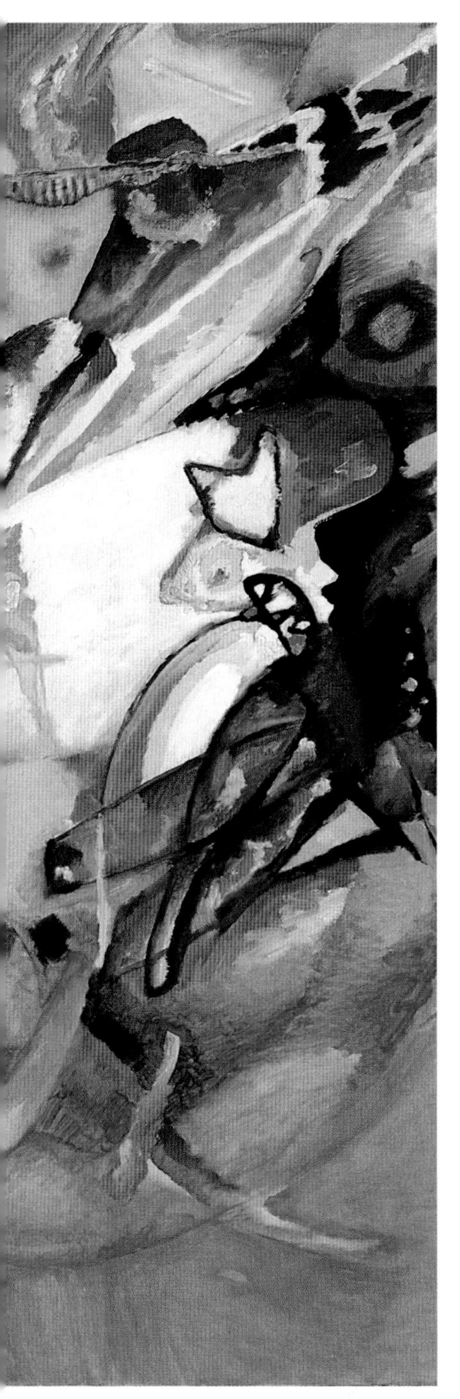

Let's zoom in closer...

Kandinsky paints the same motifs, or shapes, over and over again to lead people through his paintings. Here, the motif is a sort of oval with lines or an uneven rectangle across it. How many of these can you find?

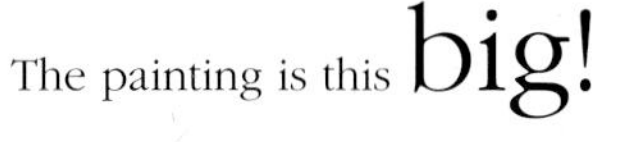

The painting is this big!

More Kandinsky "*Compositions*"...

Here are two more of the artist's *Compositions*. How do they make you feel? Do they remind you of anything? Try showing them to other people, and ask how these make them feel—are their feelings the same as yours? One piece of music might make some people feel sad, and others feel peaceful—it's the same with pictures.

Composition 8, 1923

Composition 4, 1911

Paint *to music*

Gather this equipment

together before you begin.

Music to listen to

Paintbrushes

Pens or...

... paint

Paper

1. Use a wide brush to sweep light-colored paint across the paper to give the overall mood of the piece. Let it dry. This piece was joyful.

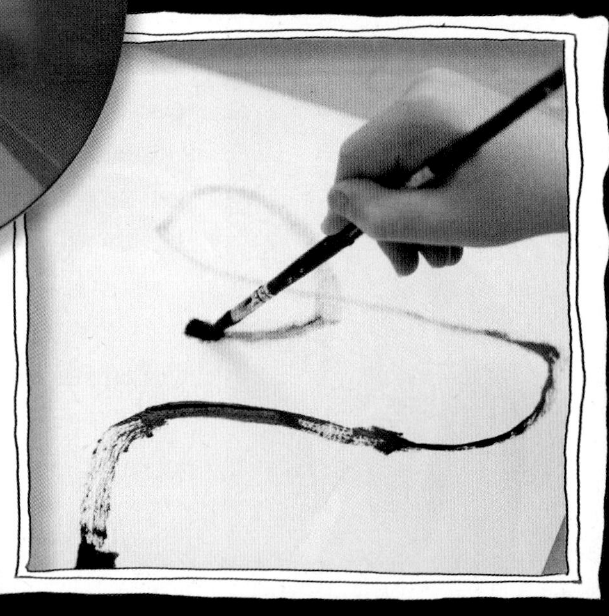

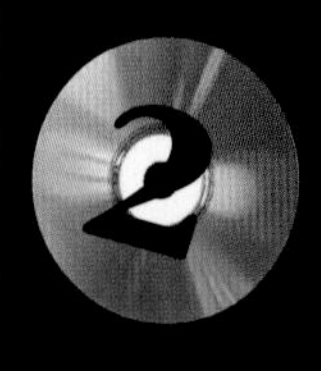

2. Across the page, paint or draw a line that suits the rhythm of the melody. Use a swirly line for a smooth rhythm, and a zigzag line for a jerky rhythm.

Tip: In music, a motif is a part of the tune that's repeated over and over again.

My art project

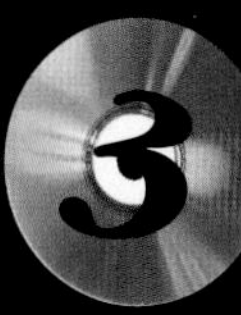

Along the line, paint a shape—a circle, perhaps—every time you hear one motif in the melody. Use other shapes if there's more than one motif.

4 Different parts of the music may inspire different feelings in you. Add shades of color around the shapes and along the lines to show these.

The finished painting. Frame it!

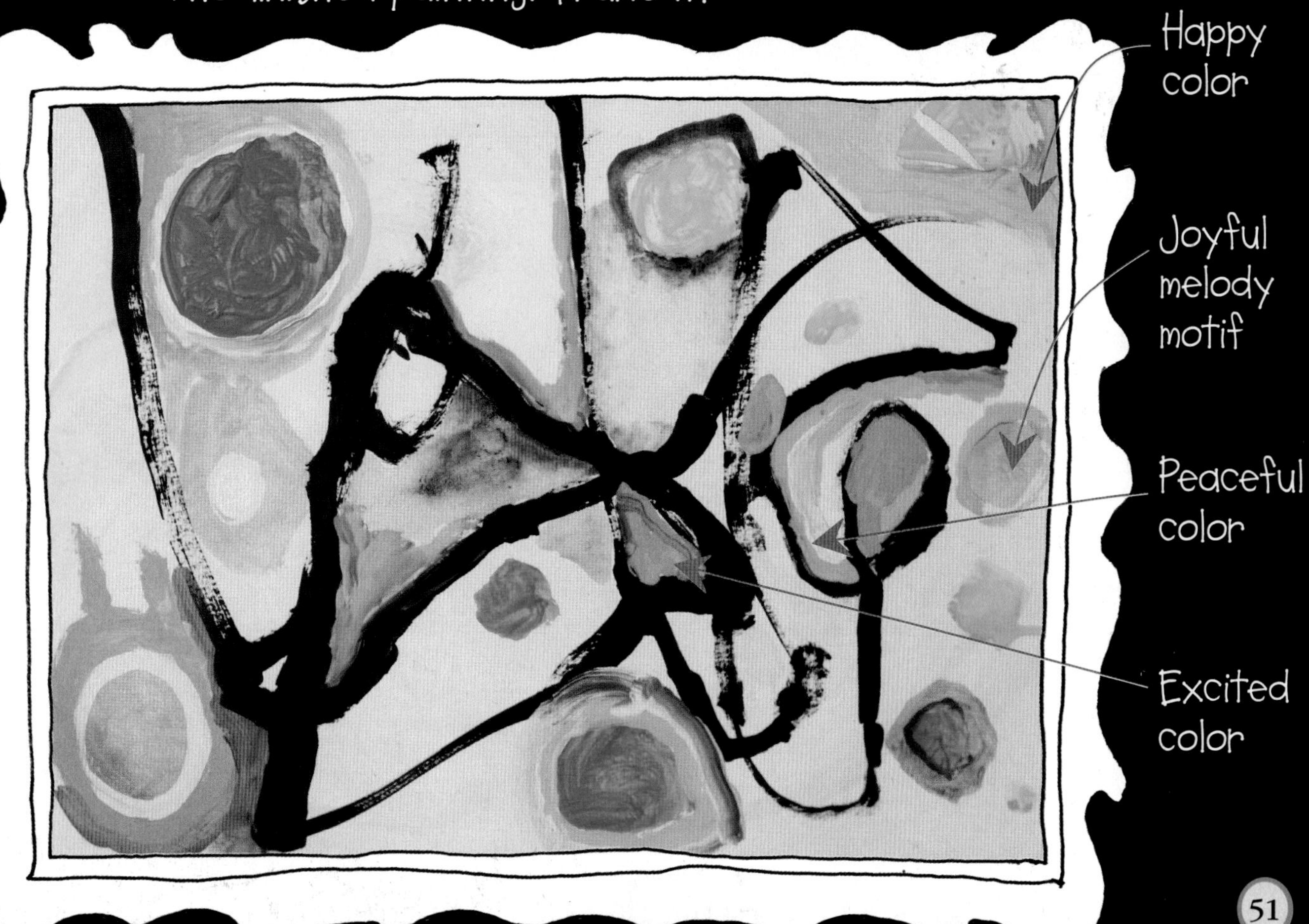

Lines and shapes

Castle and Sun
by Paul Klee, **1928,**
made with oil paint on canvas

Paul Klee (rhymes with "play") (1879–1940) was a German artist who wanted his pictures to look simple, as if a child had made them. Actually, he worked them out in great detail.

Playing with pictures

Klee created his paintings with a sense of fun—he just started drawing and let the lines grow into shapes. "A drawing," he said, "is simply a line going for a walk." Then, he moved onto colors and shades, adding and removing things until he thought the work felt balanced, or "right."

Artist

Senecio, 1922

Head lines

This picture, called *Senecio* (which means "old man"), is a bit like *Castle and Sun*, but it's different, too. There are still lots of lines and shapes, but the colors are softer, and you can see clearly what it is—a human head. What do you think this old man is like? Is he mean or kind?

Color my world

Klee loved color and made it the most important thing in his work. He was fascinated by how colors mix and feel together. Which one of Klee's colors do you like best?

This picture is all bright colors and simple shapes—squares, rectangles, triangles, and circles. Does it remind you of a castle, or maybe a row of buildings? What else can you see in it?

The painting is this big!

Klee also painted...

An Insight into the Town, 1917

Do you get the feeling of a town here? Klee's pictures don't show things clearly—they give impressions.

Paint *a town*

Gather these things

together before you begin.

Color wheel

Mixing colors				
Red	+	Yellow	=	Orange
Yellow	+	Blue	=	Green
Blue	+	Red	=	Purple

The colors red, yellow, and blue can be mixed to make all other colors. These three are called primary colors.

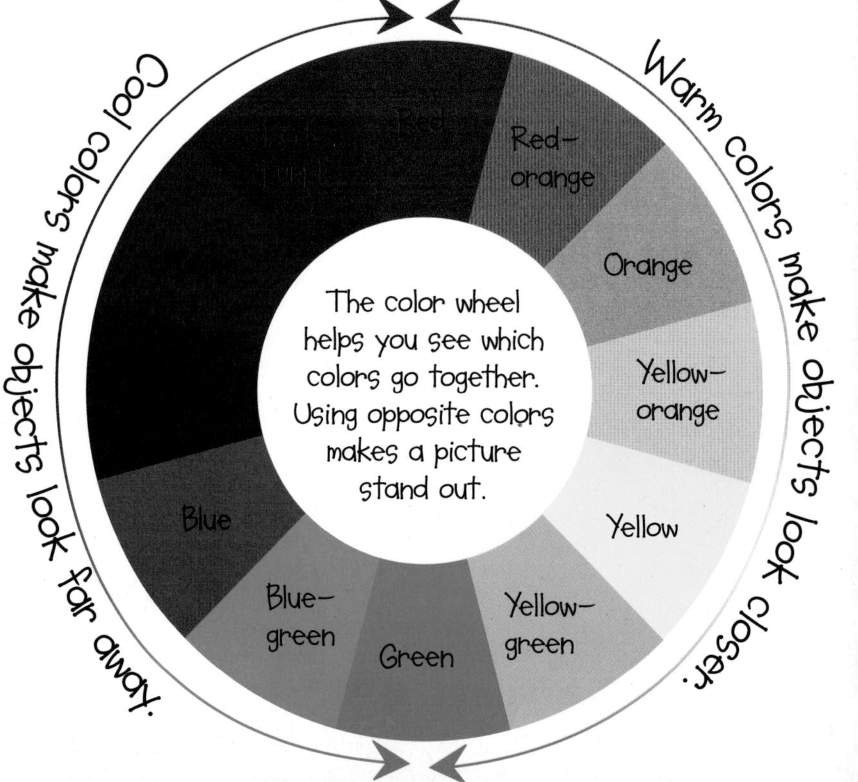

1 Draw around your shapes to create a town scene. Start from the bottom of the paper and build it up. Use triangles as windows or tops of towers.

2 Or, if you have lots of shapes cut out, use them to plan your design. Keep the shapes in place with sticky tack, then draw around them.

3 Mix the watercolors in your paintbox to create the colors you want. The color wheel will help you to choose warm or cool colors.

4 Fill each shape with a watery wash of color, keeping within the outline. While it's drying, paint a shape in another part of the picture.

5 Keep filling up the shapes. The bristles of the paintbrush need to be damp (but not wet), so wipe them on a paper towel, if necessary.

6 Now, add more dark and light paint to sections of the shapes. This will make more shape patterns and create interesting color effects.

why not try...

... getting your friends to paint a city

Add a darker wash of color for the background.
Paint a circle for the Sun.
My art project
and joining all theirs with yours?

Mosaic *magic*

Quetzalcoatl,
by Diego Rivera, **1956,**
made on the wall of Dolores Olmedo's house in Acapulco

DIEGO RIVERA (1886–1957) was a Mexican artist famous for his wall art. A mosaic is made up of tiny pieces of stone or glass held together with glue or cement.

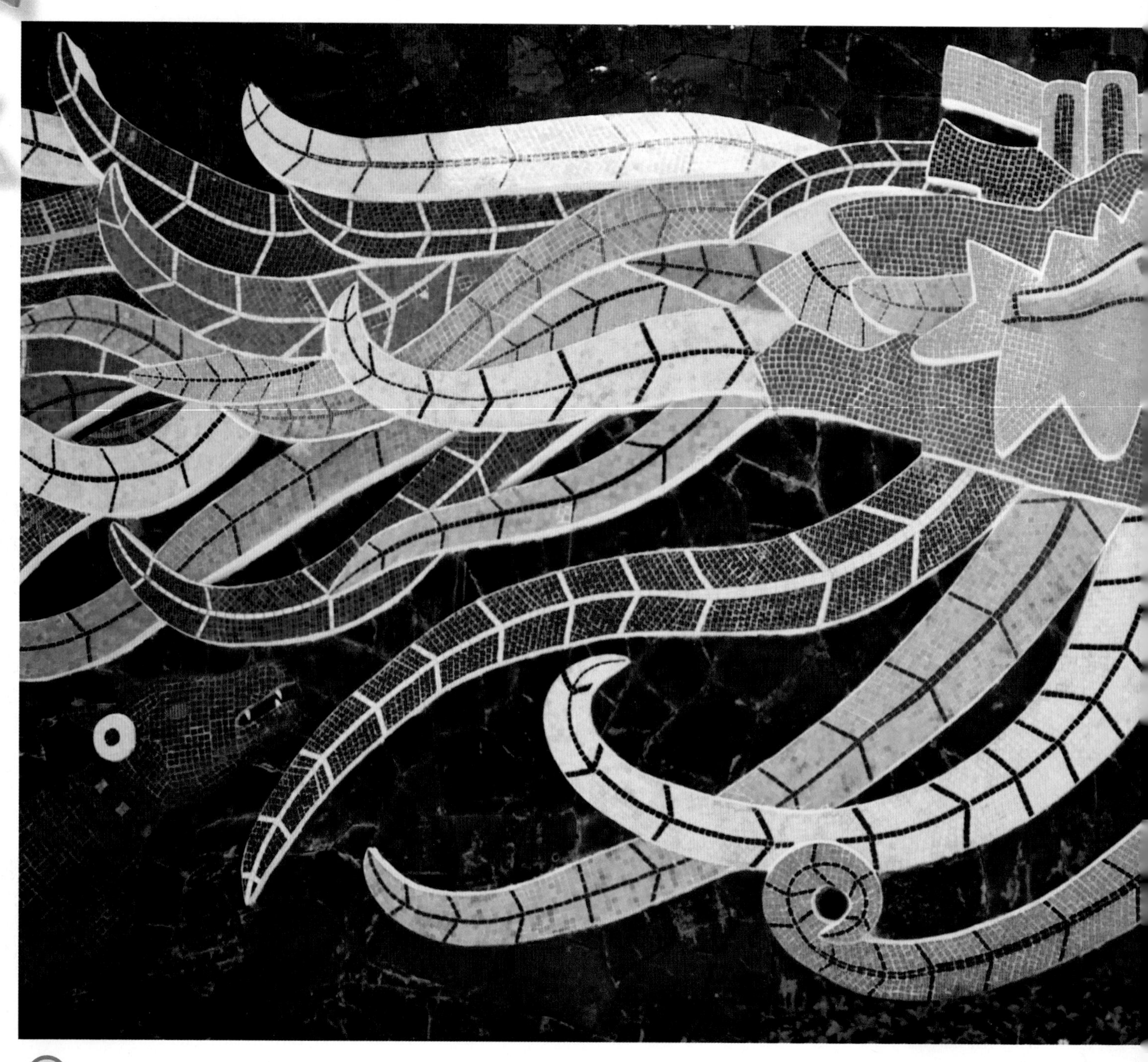

Thank you!

This mosaic was a thank you to his friend Dolores Olmedo for her support. She also let him use her house as a studio where he could work.

Let's zoom in closer...

The mosaic represents an ancient Mexican god. Up close, you can see the thousands of tiny colored stones that Rivera used.

The artist's signature

Like many artists, Rivera signed his work with his initials. He also added the year ("56") in Roman numerals LVI.

Make *a mosaic*

Collect the following equipment together, and decide what mosaic tiles you'll want to use.

1 To protect the surface of your wooden board, paint it with white paint. Wait for this to dry.

2 Draw the outline of your design onto the painted board with a pencil.

My art project

3 Plan where you'll position your mosaic tiles and decide which colors you'll use.

4 With a wooden stick, mix the tile adhesive with a little water to make cement.

5 Starting at one end, spread cement onto one small area at a time. It dries quickly, so move on to step 6.

6 Add the mosaic tiles, pressing firmly, and leaving a small gap between them for the grout.

7 Once the mosaic is finished and dry, spread grout all over it using a piece of cardboard.

8 With a damp cloth, remove the grout from the surface of the mosaic tiles while it's still wet.

Hang up your finished mosaic.

Varnish your mosaic for a shiny finish.

why not try...

... cutting around your shape? Here are two butterfly mosaics.

Use wire and beads for the antennae.

Ask an adult to cut out your shape from a piece of wood. Decorate with different-colored broken tiles.

Pebble mosaics

Busy bees

Stunning mosaics can also be made from pebbles and stones of all different colors and sizes. This mosaic of bees was created by Maggy Howarth.

Create a mosaic from an assortment of pebbles and stones collected on a beach.

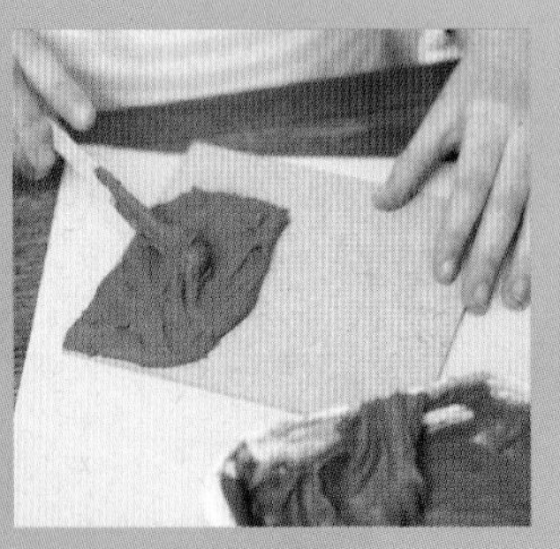

1 Spread some tile adhesive onto a plain tile using a wooden stick.

2 Press your pebbles into place with your fingers.

3 For a flower pattern like this one choose a large, flat stone for the center.

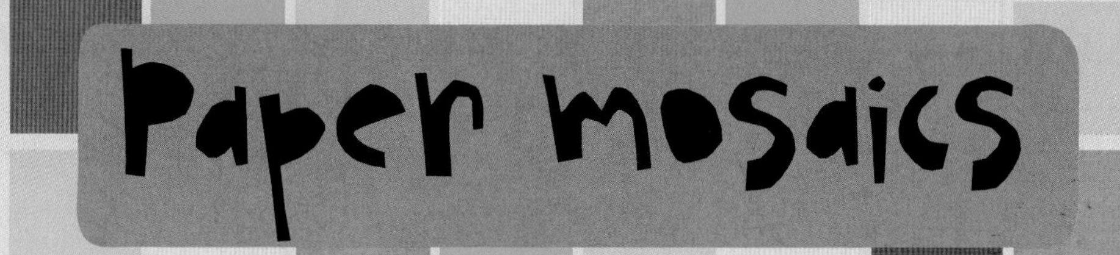

Paper mosaics

Make your own mosaic pieces from colored cardboard or paper.

Fold a large sheet into an accordion fan.

Cut the accordion fan into small squares.

Unfold each strip and tear off the squares.

Glue the pieces in place with craft glue.

Use lots of different colored squares for your fun design.

Lumps *and* bumps

HENRY MOORE (1898–1986) was a 20th-century British artist who created huge sculptures from stone, bronze, and types of plastic such as fiberglass. Many of these are abstract, or almost abstract.

Large Reclining Figure
by Henry Moore, **1951**, made from fiberglass
This is on display at Kew Gardens, London.

One of Moore's favorite themes was a lying-down figure. Here, the body is opened up so you can look through it, and the outline is smooth like a rolling hillside.

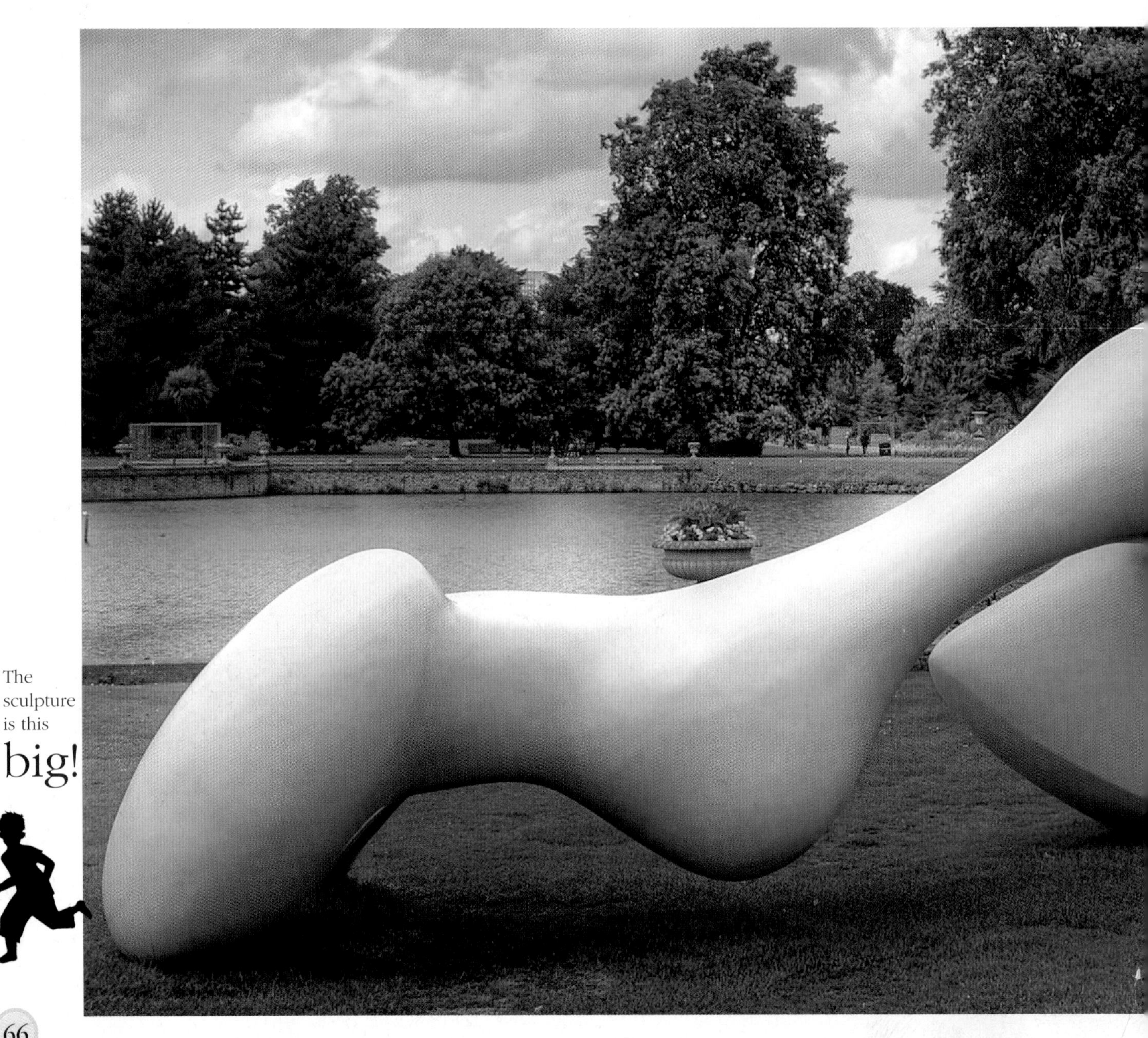

The sculpture is this big!

Henry Moore at work

Artist

Have you ever looked at a hillside and thought it looked a little like a person lying down? Moore did! He would begin by sketching lots of body shapes from different angles. He imagined the natural curves of a landscape changing into a human figure, and created holes to reveal the landscape behind the sculpture.

The sculpture is made out of a hard plastic called fiberglass, which is strong, but light.

Moore also made...

Family Group, 1947
Moore produced a number of family-group sculptures like this one.

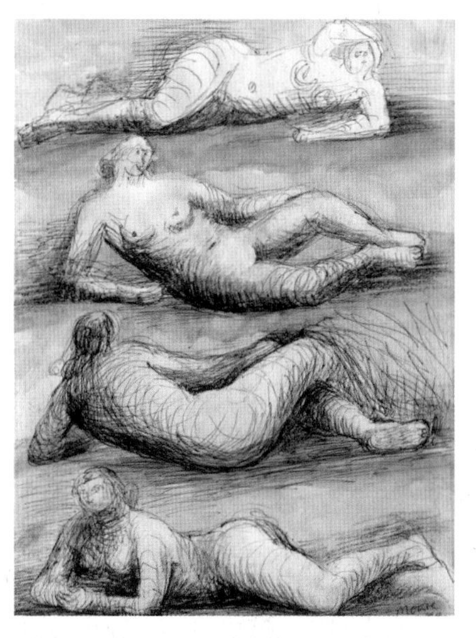

Moore's sketches for one of his sculptures of a figure lying down.

Sculpt *a figure*

Gather this equipment together before you begin. Clay can be bought from an art shop.

Colored pencil

Scissors

Paper to sketch on

Knife

Clay that can be air dried or baked in an oven

A bowl of water

A wipe-clean board

... and your hands!

My art project

1 On a sketch pad, use a colored pencil to draw a simple design of a person lying down.

2 Make a wavy outline around your figure, and add some holes to your sketch. Then cut it out.

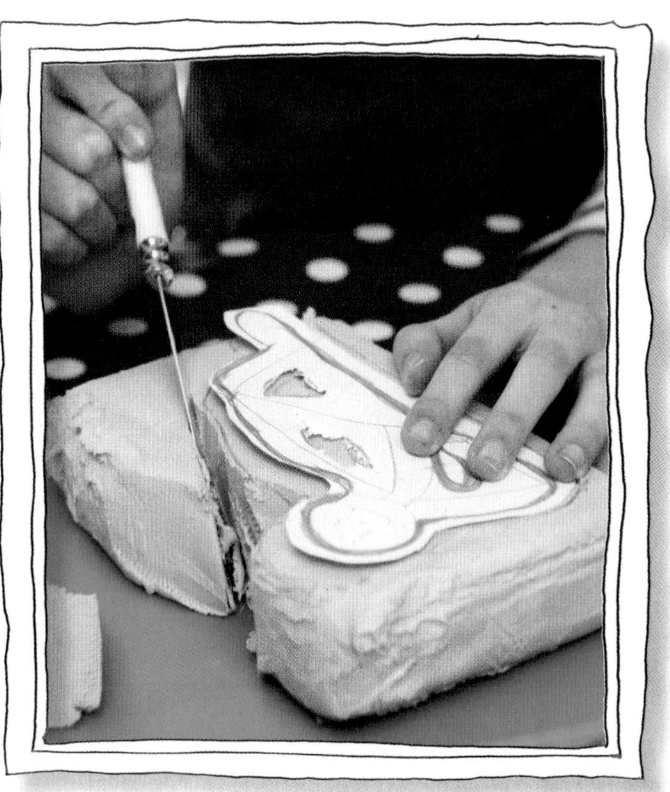

3 Place your design onto the clay and cut around with a knife. Cut out the holes.

4 Get sticky! Smooth the edges of your figure, using a little water.

Spirit art

Vigilant Owl
by Kenojuak Ashevak, **2007,**
lithograph printed on paper

KENOJUAK ASHEVAK (born 1927) is one of the best known of all Canadian Inuit artists. She creates drawings, prints, and sculptures that feature strong shapes and colors.

Beautiful birds

Ashevak uses the figure of an owl over and over in her pictures. This one is *Vigilant Owl* (2007)—vigilant means "watchful." Images from nature are important symbols in Inuit legend, but Ashevak doesn't draw owls just because they're symbols—she tries to "make something beautiful, that's all."

Lines that grow

Kenojuak Ashevak began producing art by making drawings. She never plans them—she just starts putting lines on paper and watches to see where they end up. "It just comes," she says of her work.

Ashevak's owl also appeared...

Garden Owl
In 2003, inspired by Ashevak's designs, a huge plant-and-plastic sculpture called *Conquest of Fire* was created for a garden festival in Montreal. This bright owl is part of that work.

The print is this big!

Stamp of approval
Ashevak's felt-tip drawing ***The Owl* (1969)** was chosen by the Canadian government for a special postage stamp in 1996.

Build *a bird*

Collect together lots of used household odds and ends. Look at them closely. Does anything remind you of a bird's foot, feathers, or beak? Have fun deciding!

Tip:
Ask an adult to help you cut out any parts or shapes from a plastic container.

1 Choose pieces you could use for the body, head, tail, and features. Lay them out.

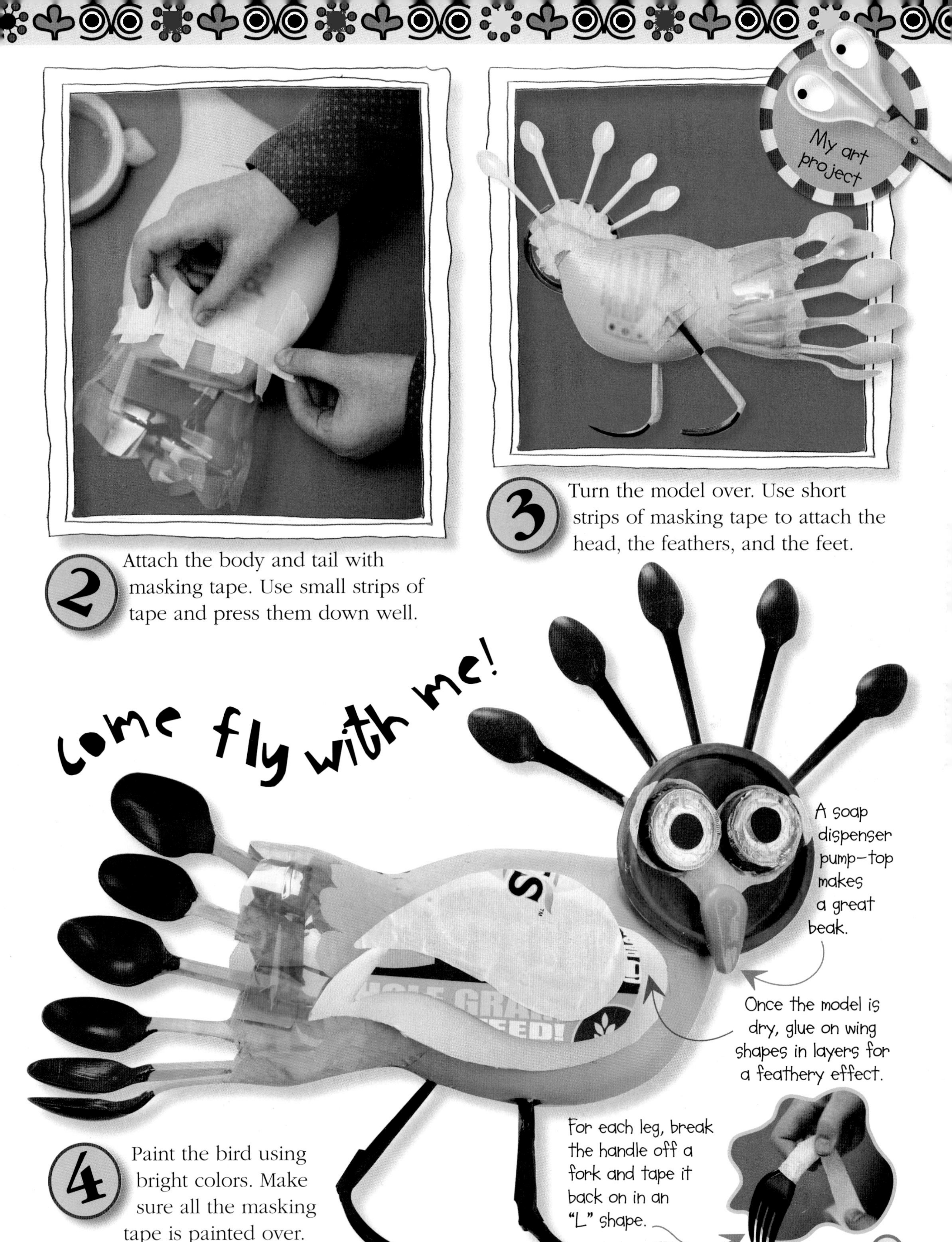
My art project
2
Attach the body and tail with masking tape. Use small strips of tape and press them down well.
3
Turn the model over. Use short strips of masking tape to attach the head, the feathers, and the feet.
Come fly with me!
A soap dispenser pump-top makes a great beak.
Once the model is dry, glue on wing shapes in layers for a feathery effect.
For each leg, break the handle off a fork and tape it back on in an "L" shape.
4
Paint the bird using bright colors. Make sure all the masking tape is painted over.

Pop art prints

Muhammad Ali
by Andy Warhol, **1978,**
paint and ink on canvas

American artist **ANDY WARHOL** (1928-1987) was one of the most famous figures of the 20th century. He began by drawing fashion illustrations, but later became one of the first (and best-known) Pop artists.

"The greatest"

In the 1960s and 70s, boxer Muhammad Ali was a popular African-American hero. He said of himself, "I am the greatest." For this portrait, Warhol started with a photo, and added lots of red, green, and black—the colors of the Pan-African flag.

Andy Warhol claimed, "Everyone will be famous for 15 minutes." His celebrity portraits weren't about real people—they were more like illustrations of fame and glamour.

The print is this big!

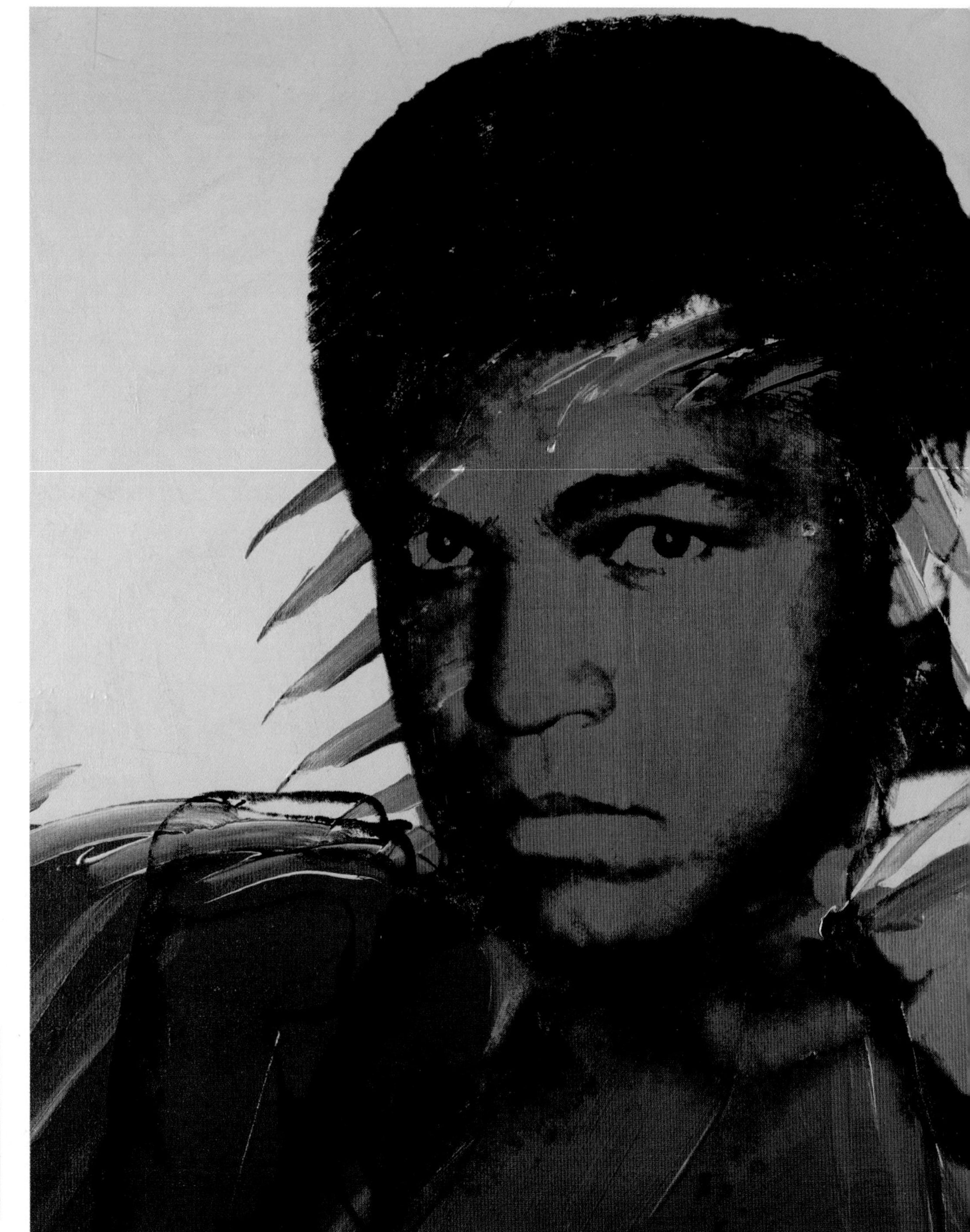

Screenprinting

Warhol made his prints using a technique called screenprinting. He chose this partly for the way it looks, but also because it suited Pop art—it was widely used for making magazines and posters.

In screenprinting, paint is forced through a fabric screen onto paper or canvas.

Pop art

Pop (short for "popular") art was inspired by the things we see around us—in advertising, on packaging, and in comics, movies, and television. In a way, Warhol's images of people (like Muhammad Ali and Marilyn Monroe) made them look like products for sale, too.

One of Andy Warhol's most famous images—***Campbell's Soup 1: Tomato,*** 1962.

Art on wheels

Mercedes-Benz 300 St. Coupé 1954, dated 1986, is one of a series called CARS. In the series, Warhol uses different Mercedes models to record automobile history.

Warhol also made...

Marilyn, 1967

Fifties movie star Marilyn Monroe was the subject of another print series. He chose the artificial colors he saw in advertising for her skin, eyes, mouth, and hair.

Pop art portrait

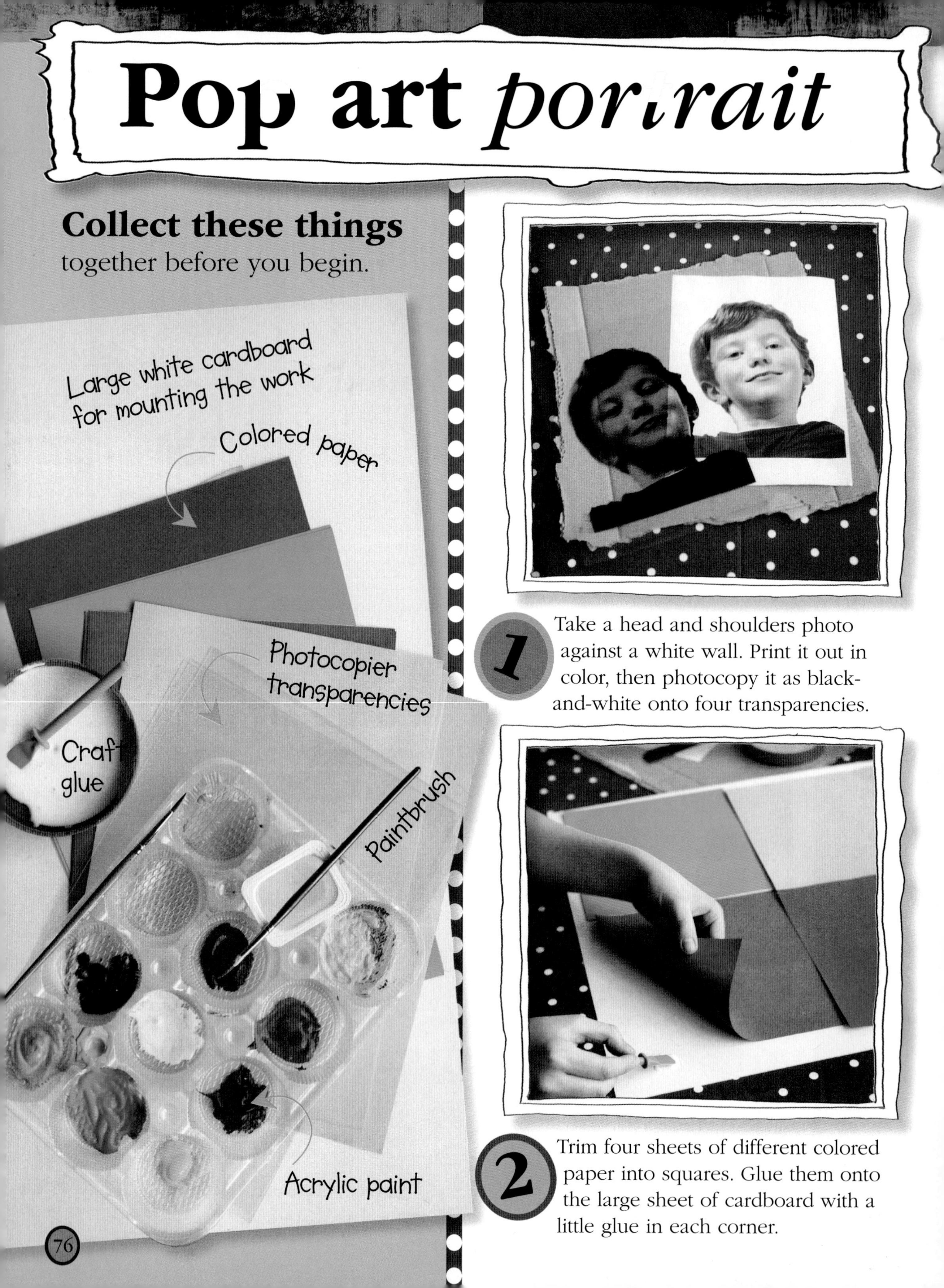

Collect these things

together before you begin.

1 Take a head and shoulders photo against a white wall. Print it out in color, then photocopy it as black-and-white onto four transparencies.

2 Trim four sheets of different colored paper into squares. Glue them onto the large sheet of cardboard with a little glue in each corner.

Tip:

Fix each transparency in place with a small dot of glue in the bottom right corner.

Trim the transparencies into squares and put one on each of the colored squares. Tear four face shapes from colored paper and place underneath the transparencies.

4

Tear strips of colored paper for the eyes, hair, and clothing to make them stand out. Lift up each transparency to put them into position. Once you're happy with your design, glue them down.

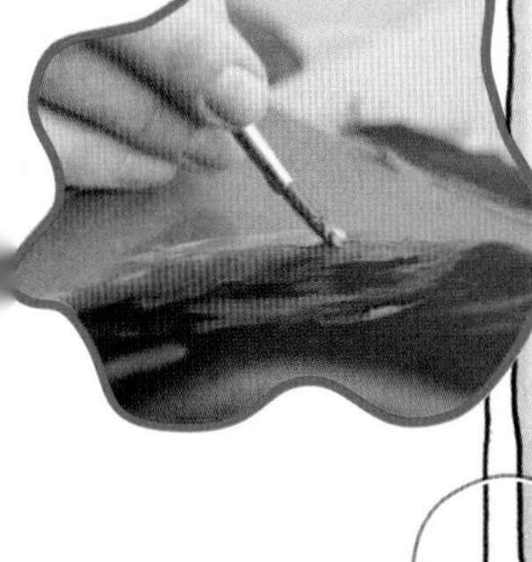

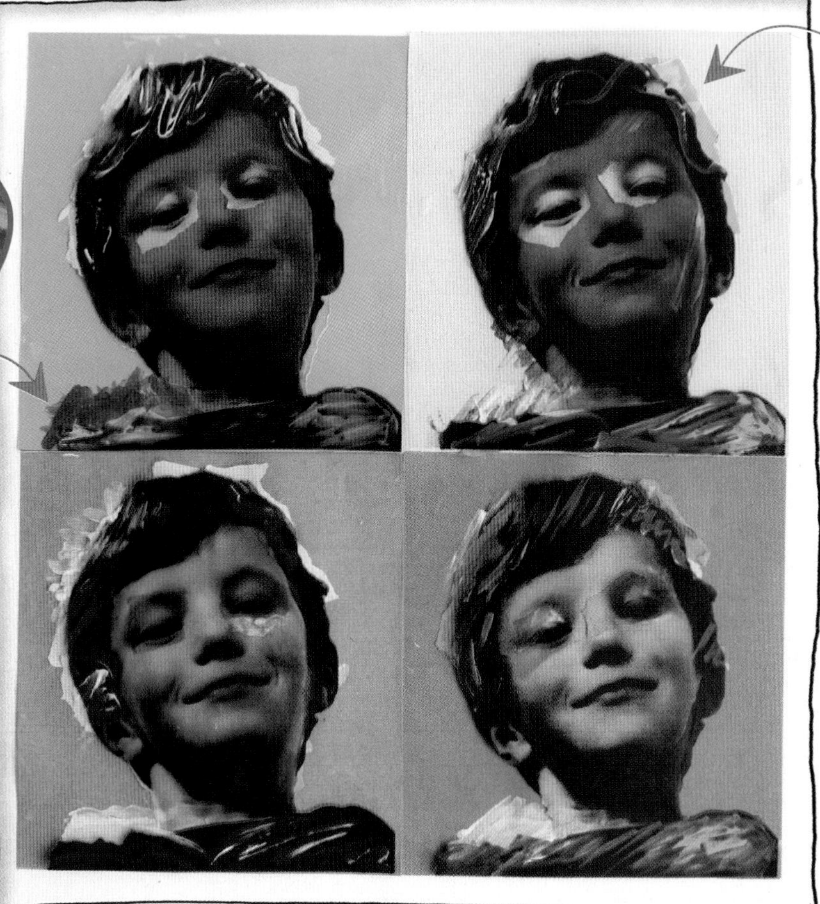

Add a few strokes of paint to the edges of the ripped paper underneath the transparencies.

Add swishes of paint to break up the black color on top of the transparencies.

Try **uploading** a photo and changing the colors on your **computer**. Some computer programs offer a "Warhol effect" option.

Famous at last! Hang your portrait in a glass frame to protect it.

Glossary

Abstract art
Art that doesn't show scenes or objects, but uses color and shape to express feelings.

Acrylic paint
A type of paint popular since the 1950s. It looks like oil paint, but it's mixed with water and dries more quickly.

Canvas
A cloth that artists paint on, usually made of linen or cotton.

Collage
A picture made by sticking assorted materials to paper or board.

Lithograph
A print in which the design is drawn with a greasy crayon on a slab of special stone.

Mask
A face covering that hides people's identity, or helps them look like someone else.

Mosaic
A picture or pattern made up of thousands of tiny pieces, usually of glass or stone.

Oil paint
Paint in which the colors are mixed with sticky oils from plants or other sources. It's a favorite with artists since it can create many different effects.

Pastel
A stick of dried paint made from powdered color. It's like a crayon, but not greasy.

Pattern
A decorative design.

Pigment
Powdered color mixed with liquid to make paint.

Pop art
A type of art that uses bold images like those in comics or advertising.

Portrait
A picture or sculpture of a person, especially the face.

Screenprint
A print made by wiping ink through a silk mesh onto paper or canvas. Parts of the mesh block the ink to make the design.

Sculpture
Art made in three dimensions, usually from materials such as stone, wood, metal, or plastic.

Shade
Darkness in a picture, sometimes used to suggest shape or distance.

Sketch
A rough drawing that acts as a plan for a piece of art.

Symbol
A sign or object that stands for something else. Australian Aborigines, for example, often use a circle to represent a waterhole.

Symmetrical
A shape that can be divided into two halves that are mirror images of each other.

Texture
The surface look and feel of a material.

Watercolor
A type of paint in which solid colors are mixed with water, then applied with a brush.

Woodblock print
A print made from a design that has been carved onto a smooth block of wood. A different wood block is used for each color required.

Index

Acknowledgments

Dorling Kindersley would like to thank Marlborough Primary school for its support and Isabelle Roché for her advice.

Models and young artists: Luma Ullah, Tommy Heap, Stanley Heap, Scarlett Heap, Kate Heap, Fiona Lock, Peter Lock, Oscar Graham-Rosser, Amber Jones, Henna Hingorani, Amanda Kamuene, Mia Marumoto Quinn, Anna Turgoose, and Hannah Moore.

The publisher would like to thank the following for their kind permission to reproduce their photographs:
(Key: a-above; b-below/bottom; c-center; f-far; l-left; r-right; t-top)

1 CGTextures.com: (Papers). Steven Moore Photography. **2 The Art Archive:** Musee d'Orsay Paris/Dagli Orti (bc). **Corbis:** The Gallery Collection (br). **Courtesy B. J. Haddad:** © 2010 Banco de México Diego Rivera Frida Kahlo Museums Trust, Mexico, D.F./DACS (tl). **3 akg-images:** Erich Lessing (tl). **The Art Archive:** Private Collection/Dagli Orti (fbl). **The Bridgeman Art Library:** Museum of Modern Art, New York, USA (bl); Private Collection/ The Stapleton Collection (ftr); Tretyakov Gallery, Moscow, Russia/© ADAGP, Paris and DACS, London 2010 (ftl). **Corbis:** © The Andy Warhol Foundation for the Visual Arts/Artists Rights Society (ARS) , New York/DACS, London 2010. (fbr); The Gallery Collection (tr). **Peter Gordon:** Reproduced by permission of The Henry Moore Foundation (br). **6 Getty Images:** Time Life Pictures. **7 Corbis:** Pierre Vauthey/Corbis Sygma (cr). **Getty Images:** The Bridgeman Art Library (t). **12-13** Courtesy of the Margaret Levi and Robert Kaplan Collection, and the artists Napanangka Lucy Yukenbarri, Napanangka Mati(Bridget) Mudgedell, Naparulla Rose Nanyuma, Napangarti Bai Bai Sunfly, Nampitjin Millie Skeen, Napanangka Tjemma (Freda) , Nampitjin Rita Kunintji. **13 Alamy Images:** Bill Bachman/© Warlayirti Artists 2000 (t). **naturepl.com:** Jouan & Rius (cr). **16 The Art Archive:** Private Collection/Dagli Orti. **17 The Bridgeman Art Library:** Private Collection/ Photo © Heini Schneebeli (r) (l). **21 Steven Moore Photography:** (cl) (c) (cr). **Hazel Terry:** (tc), Darren Millar (tcl), Fiona Horan (bcl), Lisa Wishart (bc), Melissa Connolly (bcr). **22 akg-images:** Erich Lessing (bl) (r) (tr/cherries) (tr/leaf) (tr/onion) (tr/pea) (tr/ rose bud). **23 akg-images:** Erich Lessing (tr/pear). **The Bridgeman Art Library:** Kunsthistorisches

Jungle Collage by Amber, age 10

Museum, Vienna, Austria (bl); Museo Civico Ala Ponzone, Cremona, Italy (br). **28 The Bridgeman Art Library:** Private Collection/ The Stapleton Collection (b). **28-29 The Bridgeman Art Library:** Private Collection/ The Stapleton Collection (t). **29 The Bridgeman Art Library:** Private Collection/ The Stapleton Collection (cra) (ca) (cb). **Getty Images:** Keren Su (tl). **The Hokusai Museum:** (br). **34 The Art Archive:** Musee d'Orsay Paris/ Dagli Orti. **Steven Moore Photography:** (cl). **35 Alamy Images:** The Art Gallery Collection (br). **The Art Archive:** Musee d'Orsay Paris/Dagli Orti (l). **The Bridgeman Art Library:** © Culture and Sport Glasgow (Museums) (tr). **38 La Maison du Pastel:** (br). **40 The Bridgeman Art Library:** Museum of Modern Art, New York, USA. **41 The Bridgeman Art Library:** Museum of Modern Art, New York, USA (cl) (bl); **Corbis:** The Gallery Collection (tr). **Steven Moore Photography:** (tl). **42 Steven Moore Photography:** (br). **43 Steven Moore Photography:** (tl) (tr). **44 Corbis:** The Gallery Collection. **45 The Bridgeman Art Library:** Norton Simon Collection, Pasadena, CA, USA (br). **Corbis:** The Gallery Collection (c). **Steven Moore Photography:** (tl). **46 Steven Moore Photography:** (tr) (bl). **47 Steven Moore Photography:** (tl). **48 The Bridgeman Art Library:** Tretyakov Gallery, Moscow, Russia/© ADAGP, Paris and DACS, London 2010. **49 akg-images:** © ADAGP, Paris and DACS, London 2010 (cr). **The Bridgeman Art Library:** Kunstsammlung Nordrhein-Westfalen, Dusseldorf, Germany/Peter Willi/© ADAGP, Paris and DACS, London 2010 (br); Tretyakov Gallery, Moscow, Russia/© ADAGP, Paris and DACS, London 2010 (c). **52 Corbis:** The Gallery Collection. **53 The Bridgeman Art Library:** Kunstmuseum, Basel, Switzerland/ Giraudon (cl); Mayor Gallery, London (br). **Steven Moore Photography:** (tr). **58 Courtesy B. J. Haddad:** © 2010 Banco de México Diego Rivera Frida Kahlo Museums Trust, Mexico, D.F./DACS. **59 Alamy Images:** David R. Frazier Photolibrary, Inc/© 2010 Banco de México Diego Rivera Frida Kahlo Museums Trust, Mexico, D.F./DACS. (t). **Courtesy**

Sunflowers by Mia, age 10

B. J. Haddad: © 2010 Banco de México Diego Rivera Frida Kahlo Museums Trust, Mexico, D.F./ DACS (r). **63 Steven Moore Photography:** (b). **64 Courtesy Maggy Howarth:** (t). **66 Peter Gordon:** Reproduced by permission of The Henry Moore Foundation. **66-67 Reproduced by permission of the Henry Moore Foundation:** (t). **67 The Bridgeman Art Library:** Private Collection/ Photo © Connaught Brown, London/ Reproduced by permission of The Henry Moore Foundation (br). **Corbis:** Christie's Images/Reproduced by permission of The Henry Moore Foundation (cr). **TopFoto.co.uk:** John Hedgecoe/Reproduced by permission of The Henry Moore Foundation (tl). **68-69 Reproduced by permission of the Henry Moore Foundation:** (t). **69 Steven Moore Photography:** (br). **70 Permission Dorset Fine Arts. 71 William Ritchie 2010:** (t). **Courtesy D'n'D Stamps, www.dndstamps.com:** Permission Dorset Fine Arts (br). **© Mosaïcultures Internationales de Montréal:** (c). **74 Corbis:** © The Andy Warhol Foundation for the Visual Arts/Artists Rights Society (ARS), New York/DACS, London 2010. **74-75 fotolia:** Andrii Pokaz (t). **75 Alamy Images:** Peter Huggins (tl). **Corbis:** © The Andy Warhol Foundation for the Visual Arts/Artists Rights Society (ARS), New York/ DACS, London 2010 (tr) (cl). **Photo Scala, Florence:** © 2010. Digital image, The Museum of Modern Art, New York/© The Andy Warhol Foundation for the Visual Arts/Artists Rights Society (ARS), New York/DACS, London 2010. (br). **79 Steven Moore Photography:** (t) **Jacket images:** *Front:* **Corbis:** Bettmann bl; Bruce Burkhardt (frame), bl br; Ocean tl. *Back:* **akg-images:** Erich Lessing tc; **Steven Moore Photography:** bl

All other images © Dorling Kindersley
For further information see: www.dkimages.com

Jungle Tiger by Amanda, age 9

Sunflowers by Hannah, age 9

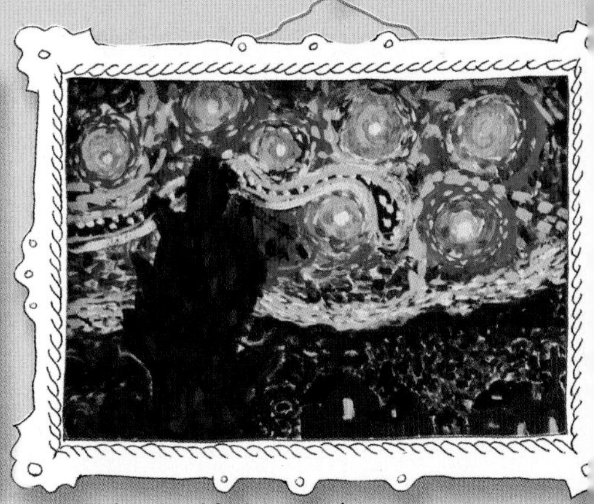

Starry Night by Anna, age 9